GOOD FISHING

in the Finger Lakes Region
and Western New York

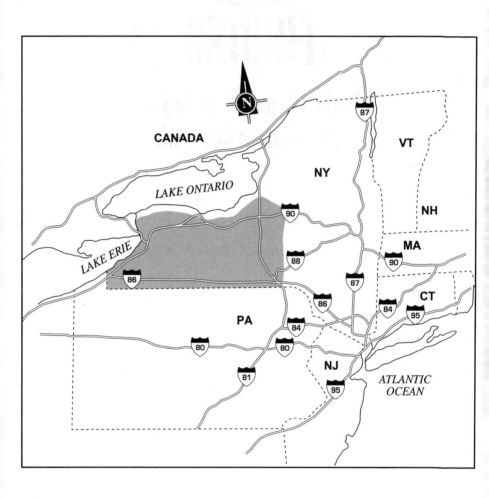

GOOD FISHING

in the Finger Lakes Region and Western New York

The Finger Lakes and other Waters,
from Oneida Lake to Chautauqua Lake

C. Scott Sampson
Editor

Maps drawn by AD•PRO Graphics
Layout by Gamut Design

Sander's
Fishing Guides, Inc.

Information products for the 21st-century fisherman

www.sandersfishingguides.com

Sander's Fishing Guides, Inc.
Amherst, New York

Sander's Fishing Guides, Inc.
P.O. Box 624
Amherst, New York 14226

Previously published under the title *Good Fishing in Western New York - The Finger Lakes and Other Waters, from Oneida Lake to Chautauqua Lake* by Backcountry Publications, Woodstock Vermont.

Printed in the United States of America

10-9-8-7-6-5-4-3-2

ACKNOWLEDGMENTS

The authors would like to acknowledge the dedicated and knowledgeable members of the fisheries staffs of the New York State Department of Environmental Conservation. Their untiring efforts are the reason we can write about GOOD FISHING IN THE FINGER LAKES REGION AND WESTERN NEW YORK. The list of professionals includes but is not limited to Clifford Creech, Thomas L. Chiotti, Les Wedge, Doug Stang, Carl Widmer, David Kosowski, William Abraham, Sr., Steve Morradian and Joseph Evans.

No less important are the fellow anglers who have shared their experiences, knowledge, and often companionship while the knowledge was gathered for these pages. They include Tony Buffa, Fred David, Leonard Lisenbee, Frank Krowiak, Paul Keesler, Don DeSio, Ransom Snyder, Jim Haviland, Jim Martino, Ernie Lantiegne, Roy Japp, Walt Burgeson, Bob Tretsky, Bill Haessner, Les Bruer, Wayne Brewer, Charlie Jensen, Bill Stokoe, Bill Reeser, Dick Waite, Deiter Kraemer, Steve Walker, Al Himmel, Dave Tooke, Rick Kinecki, Bob Janiga, Jim Keech, Will Elliott, Gordon Dietrick, Paul Maciejewski, Tom Piwowar, Leo Barus, Ray Lytle, Dave Peterson, Russell Johnson, Warren Berry, Paul Swanson, and Dave Bianchi.

Most important, however, are the wives and other family members who put up with those addicted by angling and, worse yet, writing about angling, especially Sonni Sampson, Carol Maloney, Mary Kelly, Carol Lisenbee, and Rose Barus.

WARNING!

The New York State Department of Health warns that many fish in New York waters have certain potentially harmful contaminants. You are advised to consult the New York State Department of Environmental Conservation for further details. Many of the current advisories will be seen in the DEC annual publication "New York State Fishing Regulations Guide" or can be obtained by calling 1-800-458-1158, Ext. 27815.

CONTENTS

MAPS

MAP LEGEND

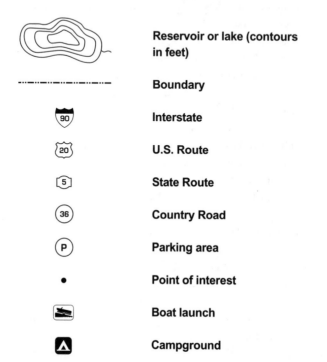

Reservoir or lake (contours in feet)

Boundary

Interstate

U.S. Route

State Route

Country Road

Parking area

Point of interest

Boat launch

Campground

No attempt was made to show all boat/canoe launches or campgrounds. Only very select points of interest are depicted on the maps in this book. Not all secondary roads are shown.

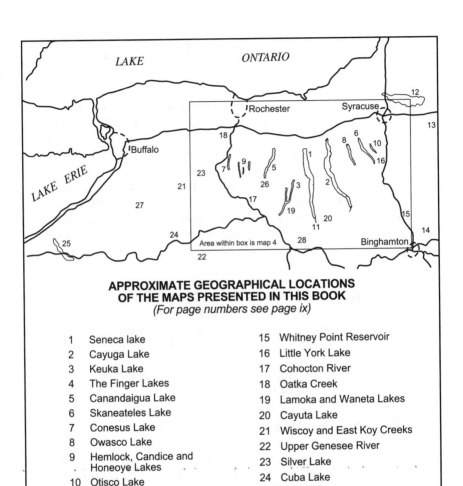

LAKE ONTARIO

LAKE ERIE

Rochester
Syracuse
Buffalo

18
23 7 9 5
26 3
17 19 11
27 20
24 28
25 22 Area within box is map 4

8 6 10
1 16
2
15
14
Binghamton

12
13

APPROXIMATE GEOGRAPHICAL LOCATIONS
OF THE MAPS PRESENTED IN THIS BOOK
(For page numbers see page ix)

ABOUT THE AUTHORS

C. Scott Sampson, editor/author, started fishing in western New York more than 40 years ago. For the past thirty years he has been reporting on these and other outdoor adventures in the FINGER LAKES TIMES and the NEW YORK SPORTSMAN as well as numerous other local and national publications.

Leo Maloney covers the outdoors for the ONEIDA DAILY DIS-PATCH, the central area of the state for NEW YORK SPORTSMAN and is a contributor or such magazines as Field and Stream and Great Lakes Fisherman. Fishing is his area of expertise, especially in central and northern New York.

J. Michael Kelly is the outdoor columnist for the Syracuse POST STANDARD. He has been published in WILDFOWL, WING & SHOT, ADIRONDACK LIFE, AMERICAN ANGLER & FLY TYER and SALMON-TROUT-STEELHEADER publications. More often than not the subjects are fly fishing or bird hunting.

Len Lisenbee is the outdoor columnist for the CANANDAIGUA MESSENGER. He filed his first hooks up on Chesapeake Bay and served as a saltwater mate for charter fishing before be was converted to fly tying and bass plugging in upstate New York.

David L. Barus, also known as Forest Fisher, is an avid angler. He syndicates a weekly outdoor column, "Rod, Gun and Game", to numerous western New York papers. He is the founder of Inland Sportsman Hotspot Fishing Map Company.

INTRODUCTION

GOOD FISHING IN THE FINGER LAKES REGION AND WESTERN NEW YORK is a working guide that will show you the angling opportunities that abound in this area of the state. It also will give you the knowledge necessary to catch fish, from trout to crappie and everything in between.

You will tour all of the Finger Lakes plus Oneida Lake and Chautauqua Lake. There also is information on a potpourri of smaller lakes and streams, each of which offers good fishing opportunity. These smaller, high-quality waters were selected based on the availability of public access and because they offer a quality fishery that is easily available to the average angler. These waters are organized by their locations in the three western administrative divisions of the New York State Department of Environmental Conservation (DEC), Regions 7, 8 and 9.

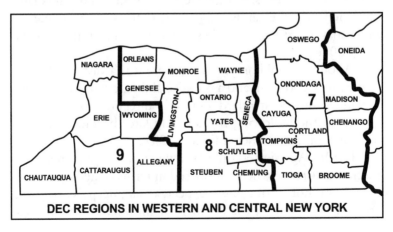

DEC REGIONS IN WESTERN AND CENTRAL NEW YORK

GOOD FISHING IN THE FINGER LAKES REGION AND WESTERN NEW YORK does not, for the most part, list private facilities for fishing access if public access is available nearby. Private facilities can change ownership, and therefore policy and pricing, from year to year, and it is our intent not to provide information that may mislead you.

You should be able to use this book as a basic guide to a successful fishing trip. You may want to supplement this information with advice available with a visit to a local bait and tackle shop, chamber of commerce, or regional office of the DEC. The bounty of waters in this region of New York awaits you.

The good fishing found in the Finger Lakes region and western New York is largely a gift of the Ice Age. The continental glaciers excavated, both with water and abrasion, the deep-water lakes we now call the Finger Lakes. The glacier also produced hundreds of smaller bodies of water as blocks of ice broke free of the main mass. These became buried in the rubble, later to melt and form many of the waters we fish today. Tully Lake near Cortland is a classic example of this geologic phenomena.

All of the western half of New York, including the Finger Lakes region, was a flat surface some 550 million year ago and was covered by a vast ocean. Deposits of silts and muds later hardened into the sandstone, shale, slate, and limestone we find today. In certain areas these deposits can be found as deep as 8,000 feet.

About 200 million year ago, there was a vast uplifting of that early sea bottom, and a pre-glacial divide started the rivers flowing from the standard southerly direction to the north. Those northerly flowing rivers would later become pathways for much of the advancing fingers of ice.

The Ice Age started only 10 million years ago, a relatively recent occurrence when considered in terms of geological history. It was not, as one might expect, a giant deep freeze, just a consistent cooling of the northern hemisphere by an average of 15 to 20 degrees. But, at higher elevations, that was enough. The most recent glacier had its birth in the area of Labrador and each year grew in thickness. At its peak, the main portion of the continental glacier was estimated by geologists to have been some 10,000 feet thick. As it eventually spread south and into the warmer Finger Lakes region, the glacier still retained a depth of nearly 2,500 feet. This mass of ice traveled at the rate of 2 to 3 feet a day and eventually reached as far south as Williamsport, Pennsylvania.

The glacier did more than just cut and plow the earth's crust, for it was combined with a significant hydraulic force equally effective in creating topographic changes. Under enough pressure, ice flows like a liquid; thus there was a washing action as well as the cutting and scraping by the solid ice and imbedded rock and rubble.

The Finger Lakes region was near the southernmost reach of the glacial lobes. As a result, the area was not scrubbed flat. Instead the ice reached out, much in the manner of fingers of a giant, outstretched hand. The lobes followed the paths of least resistance, which was in the river beds. Between the lobes the highlands were left intact.

Gorges such as Watkins Glen or Taughannock Falls were, back then, the locations where a river fell off the edge of the glacial cut. They were rivers left hanging in mid-air as the glacier moved past. As the ice receded, the falling water cut back the edges, forming these gorges as it passed through the relatively soft rock. Today, the delta that is the picnic area at Taughannock State Park, where some superb fishing is available off the point, is the result of this erosion. A depth finder easily records the nearly straight drop from the lake shore to the depths of the lake where the edge of the glacier moved past, cutting the channel in a manner similar to a giant steam shovel. Originally, these edges were not tapered but instead were a shear drop. Only time has softened and rounded the edges.

Time and fisheries management have combined to improve what the Ice Age started, all to the benefit of anglers. The good old days were never this good, and the future of our fishing appears brighter still.

C. Scott Sampson

PART I

THE FINGER LAKES
by C. Scott Sampson

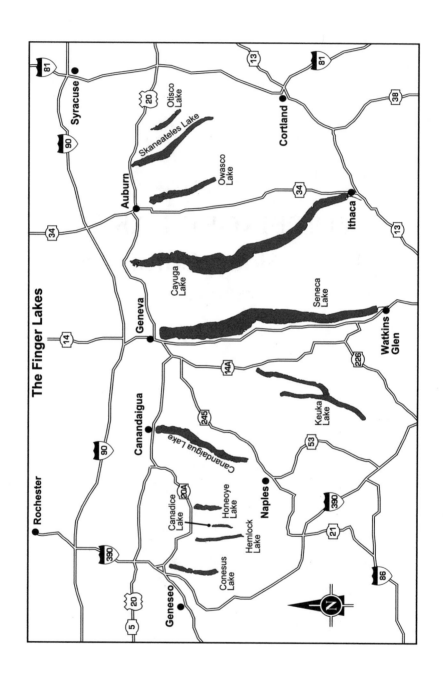

The Finger Lakes

Chapter 1
SENECA LAKE
by C. Scott Sampson

The eight-foot light action downrigger rod had a perfect arch. Only the tip jerked in a steady, even movement signaling the head-shaking of a good lake trout on the other end. I pumped the rod while fishing partner Ray Wolinski stood by with the landing net.

He followed my instructions to extend the handle in order to reach over the 70 horsepower motor and pick up the prize. We really should have cleared the other three downriggers to make room for this fish, but we had instead dropped the speed of the troll to idle in-gear. We were playing the lazy game of bringing the fish through the lines and over the stern of the boat. Even with a good fish you can normally put the motor into neutral at the last minute and back into gear as soon as the fish is safely aboard – and still not tangle the other set lines.

We both were getting more excited as the lake trout surfaced off the stern. It had taken a good ten minutes to bring it up from the depths and it was now flashing its silver and gray-green colors as it attempted to get away.

Before I could speak Wolinski had one foot in the outboard engine splash well while trying to gain more of an extension to the fish. I couldn't decide if I was more concerned with him falling overboard or with landing the fish, so I kept my mouth shut. When he netted the fish, I released the tension on the rod and grabbed him. Both came tumbling into the boat.

I had to laugh at Wolinski laying on the deck of the boat and me trying to control one of the larger lake trout I have taken in recent years. I slipped a large-hooked boat scale under the jaw and it pulled the marker to 11¾ pounds.

"Do you want this one?" I asked. He shook his head no, still laughing at himself and hardly able to speak. We both were well aware that the best eating lake trout are in the two to three-pound class. I looked for fin clips or other identifying marks, then slipped the trout carefully over the side.

Not counting the Great Lakes, Seneca Lake is the deepest inland body of water east of the Rockies. Largely because of its depth – 618 feet at the maximum and an average of 291 feet – it has one of the premiere cold water fisheries in New York State. It is also one of the largest of the Finger Lakes with 66.6 square miles of surface area and 75.4 miles of shoreline. It is fed by two principal tributaries, the famed Catharine Creek at the south end and Keuka Lake Outlet on the west side at Dresden. The outlet from the lake is through the Seneca-Cayuga Canal.

An angler fishing the 38-mile-long lake for the first time is almost overwhelmed. Where do you begin when you can't even see the other end? Make no mistake, Seneca Lake is big water. But, its fishing can be broken down by available species into manageable areas of water, and that makes it both easier to understand and fish.

Seneca Lake is perhaps most famous for its lake trout, and the wide distribution of this fish makes it a good starting point.

Long before fishing derbies became popular, Seneca Lake anglers and the city of Geneva, which lies along the lake's northern shore, began to tout the resource by calling itself the National Lake Trout Capital of the World. In 1963, the first National Lake Trout Derby was held over Memorial Day weekend. The years of derby history support the claim to that title, and the National Lake Trout Derby sends out a message that is loud and clear: New York State, and Seneca Lake in particular, has quality cold water fishing.

The derby prize money is modest by comparison to many

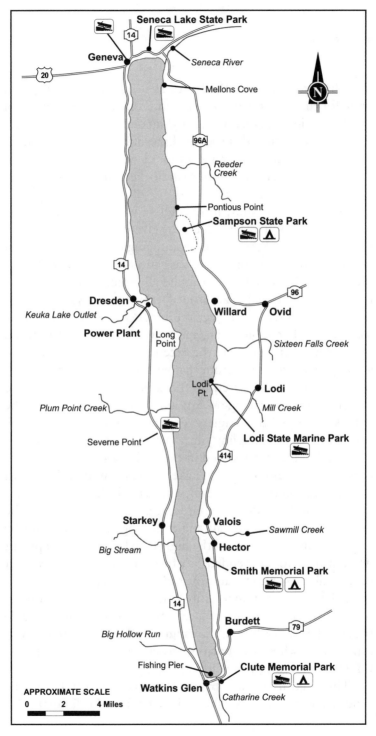

Figure 1.1   Seneca Lake

other fishing contests; $29,325 in cash including a $5,000 grand prize for the largest trout or salmon. Perhaps the real value of the derby is in perpetuating the angling traditions and the friendships shared during this special three-day weekend. The contest annually draws just over 2,000 anglers, each with the dream of catching the largest trout or landlocked salmon and collecting the grand prize.

Grand prize or not, most anglers will catch trout. The number brought to scale will, on any given year, break the 2,000 mark with most of the smaller trout being released. The largest lake trout to capture the event was caught in 1969, a lake trout that tipped the scale to 17 pounds, 13 ounces. Even though it is called the National Lake Trout Derby, the rules of the event have been changed to reflect the broader fishery and include landlocked salmon, brown and rainbow trout as well as lake trout.

Derby winning fish are the exceptions. Day-in and day-out angling produces a lake trout that will average 3 pounds. Rainbow trout will more often tip the scale at over 4 pounds and brown trout will average 4.5 pounds says the data from the diaries of cooperating anglers. For those same anglers, it took about 1½ hours of angling time to catch a legal salmonid.

Angling techniques used in the derby, and typical of what is used year-round on Seneca Lake, range from still fishing with dead or live bait to downrigging with artificial lures. Wire handlines and multi-leader Seth Green rigs are also popular. The derby has been won by an angler fishing off a dock and by anglers using the newest of the high-tech boats and equipment while fishing for suspended fish from the surface to 250 feet deep while trolling in water over 600 feet deep.

Lake trout are temperature oriented fish. And no matter what method of angling you use, the objective should be to present the bait or lure in the range of 48 degree water. If you can do that where the bottom structure meets the preferred water temperature, you will find success.

The majority of lake trout fishing is concentrated in the central and northern waters of the lake from Lodi north. But that is not to say good lake trout fishing is not available in the southern, steep-sided portions of the lake toward Watkins Glen. The northern concentration of angling has more to do with the fishing access to Seneca and available services for anglers than a concentration of fish. Most boat gas, marina repair, bait and other angler services are concentrated in the Geneva or Watkins Glen areas. Few support services will be found between these points.

On the north shore, the City of Geneva offers a free launch at its chamber of commerce. The Seneca Lake State Park marina and launch is available in the northeast sector of the lake at the beginning of the Seneca-Cayuga Canal. Fourteen miles to the south, off Route 96A, is Sampson State Park and Marina, the largest facility on the lake.

Sampson State Park has, in addition to a 123-berth marina, 245 full-service campsites that are ideal for anglers planning an extended stay. It also is central to some of the best fishing in the lake. Both the area in front of the park and the area on the opposite shore known as Dresden are year-round potential hotspots for trout.

Nine miles south of Sampson off Route 414 is Lodi State Marine Park. Small by comparison to Sampson it offers no camping but does have seasonal dockage for boats up to 25 feet and two launch ramps. This facility is administered by the Sampson Park staff and reservations and questions should be directed to the Sampson State Park office.

Between Lodi and Watkins Glen is the municipal facility of Smith Park at Hector. However, the approaching roads and "beach" launch limits the size of craft that can safely use this facility.

Clute Memorial Park in Watkins Glen has recently upgraded its access to the lake. This launch for many years was nothing more than a mud bank plus some adjacent parking on the canal portion of Catharine Creek. It now has a double launch ramp with docks and cement pads that will allow you to launch without getting your feet wet.

The steep sides along the southern portion of the lake are simply not conducive for development of launch facilities or even on-shore cottages in many instances. Going north along the western shore, off Route 14 at Severne Point, is the newest public access to the lake. This double ramp with floating docks is 13 miles up the lake from Watkins Glen. There are no other public facilities on the west side of Seneca. However, a private fee-launch at Roy's Marina, six miles south of Geneva, is an important entrance to the lake, especially during the winter months when open water fishing for lake trout takes place and other access is restricted. The Belhurst hole is just northeast of Roy's and is a popular lake trout hotspot for year-round fishing.

Lake trout, except in the spring and fall of the year, are deep water fish. An angler will do well to remember the rule of 90 when fishing here. When in doubt, fish at a depth of 90 feet. That holds true whether you are fishing with a live ale-wife, locally known as sawbelly, or trolling with downriggers and the popular silver plated Sutton spoons. If you have no idea where the fish are and don't have a graph to chart the location, you might try a multi-leader rig called a Seth Green or thermocline system. These terminal rigs are fished with heavy duty boat rods and big level-wind reels often loaded with steel line. There may be as many as five monofilament leaders at-tached to the steel line. These carry the baits or lures. Most often the lures are silver plated spoons. The leaders are set ev-ery 15 to 20 feet from the end of the line, which carries up to 48 ounces of lead to assist in taking the offerings to the depths where the fish are. The leaders will normally be loaded with flut-ter spoons, but they may also be baited with Hemlock spinners and live bait including sawbellies or rainbow smelt that are so popular in the spring of the year.

Deiter Kraemer with lake trout (left) and brown trout taken from Seneca Lake on small silver spoons trolled off downriggers in the central portion of the lake.

Still fishing with sculpin, or tom cats as they are more often called, will produce lake trout from the shallows in the spring of the year. The trout move in to the shallows in late April and May and feed on these creatures.

With any live bait fishing for lake trout you cannot be over anxious. You must give the trout the opportunity to pick up the bait and run with it before the fish feels any resistance. The trout will eventually stop and swallow the bait, and then move off looking for more food. During the second run is the time for you to close the bail and set the hook. Live bait is fished with an open spool on a spinning rod. The line is held in place by looping it under a light rubber band placed around the rod blank or handle. The weight used to take the bait to the bottom, be it 20 or 90 feet below the surface, is an egg style sinker rigged so the line can slide through the hole without the fish feeling resistance.

Wire-line fishing, or pulling copper as it is called locally, is somewhat unique to the Finger Lakes and lake trout fishing. It requires a hand-line of copper trolling wire, approximately 30 pound test, that you use to take your lure to the bottom. The Pflueger single-fixed-hook spoon in size four or five used to be the standard, but you can find anglers using Twin Minnow or spoons such as the Geneva 66 or Blade Runner. The idea is to bounce the artificial lure on the bottom, stirring up the mud, much like a bait fish or even another lake trout might do when looking for food.

This is the same enticement you are looking to create when you use flashers or lake troll systems with small flutter spoons at the terminal end. If the revolving blades are not ticking the bottom you are not catching fish. Modern downrigger anglers also will bounce their bomb (downrigger weight) and use diving type lures such as the Flatfish or Fireplug to dig into the bottom behind the bomb.

Seneca Lake lake trout is the strain of this species most often used for stocking throughout New York State. The lake is home to the brood stock. Each fall, DEC biologists gill net to collect the eggs of the mature trout that gather in the depths off Peach Orchard Point in the southern waters where their ancient spawning grounds are located. In spite of the trout's attempts at procreation, Seneca depends on stocking for its massive trout populations. Seneca enjoys an annual stocking in access of 150,000 salmonids per year. But lake trout stocking is being reduced because of increased natural reproduction, which is thought to be associated with increased water clarity. Rainbow populations are all native fish.

Seneca has produced 15 pound brown trout. While that is not an exaggeration, it has only been in the years since 1983, after lamprey control was implemented in Seneca, that the brown trout has had the opportunity to grow past its second year. The predatory lamprey also affected other salmonid species, and in its more abundant days even attacked northern pike and bass.

The brown trout responded immediately to reduced numbers of lampreys. Browns are ferocious feeders, as evidenced by the specimen taken by Jan Krowiak and her husband Frank. They were fishing the east side of the lake and pulling a Rapala off a planer board while working water three to five feet deep. The brown would later tip the scale to 7.58 pounds and take that division in the 1987 National Lake Trout Derby. The real significance of that fish was not seen until an autopsy was performed on it, as is usually done with winning fish to assure everything is in order. The brown had 22 whole or partially digested sculpin in its stomach and it had already belched up two more when it was first brought to the scale. Yet, that same fish had been willing to eat an F-9 Rapala.

Seneca's brown trout population once included the seaforellen, a strain that in certain European waters has grown in excess of 50 pounds; the experiment failed. Landlocked salmon are a recent addition to the cold water fishery and add variety to the angling pleasures.

Rainbow trout are not currently stocked in Seneca. The lake has a significant population maintained by natural reproduction

that takes place mainly in Catharine Creek. Spring run rainbow fishing is a favorite activity on April 1, not only in this creek but in many of the lesser streams that enter Seneca. Drifting an egg sack can produce a fish of three to four pounds, but a rainbow of up to 10 pounds might be possible in Catharine.

There is little question that trout fishing is the number one angler choice on Seneca Lake, but it is difficult to say whether smallmouth bass or yellow perch is in second place. Perch are the target fish of anglers in both the spring and fall of the year when they can be caught in and along the weedlines in 15 to 40 feet of water. These are not the small panfish that you find in most ponds. A Seneca Lake yellow perch, sometimes called a jack perch, can weigh up to three pounds. That is an exceptional fish, but an average perch should exceed one pound. If you get into a school of smaller perch, move. A perch of under a pound is a waste of your minnows.

Successful perch fishing along the weedlines of Dresden, Pontious Point, Glass Factory Bay, Kashong or Mellon's Cove requires a quiet approach. Bill Stokoe, a professional perch angler (it is legal to sell these fish) uses an electric motor to make his final approach to a weed line. That, says Stokoe, makes all the difference in the world.

He casts minnows or jigs tipped with minnows on an ultralight rod. His line is yellow to help him detect the strike. He uses number six gold hooks tied on three-inch loops to keep the baits close to his main line so they will slip through the weeds more easily. His minnows are hooked through the eyes so they do not come off as easily as when lip hooked. He also uses the lightest bell-type sinker necessary to take the bait to the bottom. In 15 feet of water that would be ⅛ to ¼ ounce. When he is fishing 40 and 50 feet deep he will increase the weight to as much as ½ ounce. If he does not get a strike, he reels the baits back very slowly.

The perch are schooled in the spring and fall, and if you don't start catching them right away, move. You need to find a school and then, if possible, stay with it. Filling a five-gallon pail in a couple of hours is possible on a good day.

While there are largemouth bass in the northern and southern shallows of the lake the majority of the water is smallmouth habitat. The steep sides of the lake limit the size of the weed beds, but the rock rubble created as the banks have given way is ideal habitat for this species. Using crankbaits on light line for less visibility in the clear water conditions is a typical fishing pattern for the spring. You have to get the lure or bait down to the fish. Drifting with crayfish or fathead minnows in 18 to 30 feet of water is a favorite summer activity, and several fishing guides specialize in this type of fishing.

An early B.A.S.S. tournament was held on Seneca Lake and Paul Elias won the event with limits of smallmouth caught by "kneelin and reelin" off Dresden. That is a technique where you thrust the rod deep into the water to increase the diving depth of your crankbait to reach the fish. Most of the other anglers elected to make the nearly fifty-mile run from Watkins Glen, the full length of Seneca out the canal and through three locks to fish the largemouth bass of Cayuga Lake. A violent storm on the final day pushed most of those anglers into the canal as ten-foot waves tried to sink those who remained on the lakes.

Look for structure near weedlines and you will find both bass and perch.

Northern pike in Seneca Lake are an enigma. There have been years when a half-dozen pike over 20 pounds were caught, and other years when anglers report no pike at all. Pollution control has continued to limit the weed lines in Seneca Lake, and as a result there is less pike habitat. Few anglers in recent years have targeted northern pike in Seneca Lake. Most are caught incidental to bass and perch fishing or while fishing for trout in the shallows with bait.

Warm water fishing success, including an abundance of panfish and brown bullhead (no crappie), is generally associated with the weedlines and shore-related structure. Trout and salmon, however, will more often be found suspended in the lake proper. In summer the lake stratifies and a thermocline is established, separating the warm surface waters from the colder and less oxygenated deeper waters. You will find lake trout just below or in the thermocline and the rest of the salmonoid species above it.

Identifying a thermocline is easy. It is marked by a rapid change in water temperature, at least four degrees in a column of water three feet thick. If you have a sensitive graph the thermocline may also show up on that instrument as a "line of interference" signal. The signal is caused when the sonar reflects off the algae trapped in the thermal layer. Before the water stratifies you will find lake trout scattered at depths from 30 to 120 feet below the surface. That is one of the reasons the multi-leader boat rod system is so popular.

If you are trolling for suspended trout, use light flutter spoons in the relative size of the available bait. In the spring that may be the small Stinger spoons, Sutton 31, etc. As the summer progresses move to larger spoons such as the Sutton size 44. Silver plated spoons were for many years a Finger Lakes rule. But now successful anglers easily mix colors with the traditional silver finish.

Brown trout are most often concentrated in the southern waters of the lake in the spring of the year, but at this time they will seek the warmest water available. Browns over 15 pounds have been caught by casting off Long Pier at Geneva. The Geneva seawall along the north shore and Seneca Lake State Park are other shore fishing access points where good spring fishing can be found. Trout come into the shallows to feed on smelt and other bait. Other shore angling can be successful from the marina seawall at Sampson, the park point at Lodi or along the channel of Catharine Creek as it enters Seneca Lake though Clute Memorial Park.

While brown trout are available from shore the majority of the fish will be caught by long line trolling with stickbaits (such as the Rapala) 150 or even 200 feet behind your boat. The use of side planer trolling aids have also added brown trout to the angler's box. As the surface water warms above the 55 degree mark, use deeper diving lures or trolling devices such as the Dipsy Diver to take your lure down and away from the boat.

The best brown trout waters seem to be associated with the shallows at either end of the lake or in areas such as Dresden where a hot water discharge from the oil-fired electric plant attracts the fish.

Rainbow trout can be caught using similar trolling methods, and spoons are as effective as stick baits. In the spring of the year concentrate your efforts off creek mouths, even the small tributaries. Later in the year the rainbows will be suspended over deep water in the central portions of the lake.

DEC Fisheries Biologist David Kosowski, the person in charge of the management of Seneca Lake, perhaps sums up the fishing in this Finger Lake the best when he says, "The good old days are now."

CHAPTER 2
CAYUGA LAKE
by C. Scott Sampson

T he hole in the weeds was two feet across. The frog-colored Lucky 13 landed at the edge, its hooks reaching for the vegetation to hang me up again. That seemed to be the order of the day: cast, haul the lure back with 10 pounds of weeds, then do the whole thing over again. The plug never reached the first weed.

All I could see was green, and I felt the power of a four-pound-plus bass. The head-shaking run did not last long. Between the line, the extra hooks on the lure, and the bass had quickly locked itself in the same weed growth that frustrated my casting. It was a kind of Catch 22. This area was the best for catching, but not the best for fishing. It was the best habitat for the bass, but the weeds left a hooked fish helpless and unable to really fight the angler.

I was fishing the north end of Cayuga Lake in the channel known as Demont Creek. It runs parallel to the north side of the railroad dike. I used the net and the canoe paddle to cut my trophy free of the weeds. It was just one of the seemingly unlimited numbers of lunker largemouth bass that inhabit this area of the lake.

Cayuga claims the title of largest of the Finger Lakes, although this is challenged in several official sources. Within DEC records, the lake is listed as 42,956 surface acres while Seneca is calculated at 43,343 surface acres. Another official source lists Cayuga as 66.87 square miles and 84.8 shore miles as compared to 66.61 square miles of surface water and 75.4 miles of shoreline for Seneca. After fishing both waters for more than 40 years, I really don't care. They are both large, productive bodies of water, each with its own personality, beauty, moods and quirks. They are truly "sister" waters.

Cayuga is shallower than Seneca, with an average depth of 181 feet and a maximum of 435 feet. That is more than sufficient for trout and salmon, though Cayuga has a distinct advantage in that nearly 25 percent of its water is classified in the littoral zone, water which is less than 20 feet deep. Because of this combination of deep and shallow water, Cayuga offers the greatest fishing diversity of any of the Finger Lakes.

In the northern shallows the largemouth bass is king, with crappie, northern pike, pickerel and perch also readily available. As you move south, the smallmouth bass, rainbow, brown, lake trout and landlocked salmon will be counted in the angler's

Shore fishing along the deep water edges of the delta at Taughannock Falls State Park. This is a popular fishing area, especially in the colder months of the year.

creel. There are also many less popular species including the channel catfish, American eel and carp. The New York State record for the American eel was caught in Cayuga Lake in 1986 by Larry Manino. It weighed 7 pounds, 14 ounces.

Each June, Seneca Falls hosts its International Carp Derby. The tongue-in-cheek event offers a lot of family fun, cash prizes totalling more than $1,000 and, typically, some 35-pound-plus winners.

Cayuga Lake is the catch basin for 814 square miles of watershed, the largest of any of the Finger Lakes. It also picks up the outflow of Seneca Lake via the Seneca-Cayuga Canal. A half-dozen major tributaries feed into the lake at the Ithaca area, including the Cayuga Inlet, Fall, Salmon and Taughannock Creeks. These are important spawning grounds for smelt as well as salmonids.

Like most of the Finger Lakes, Cayuga is also fed by dozens of smaller streams which are important to the spring fisheries but which often go dry in the summer months. Smelt dippers often find more success dipping in water they can jump across than in the larger and busier streams such as Salmon or Taughannock Creeks. The mouths of these same small waters are also magnets for salmon, rainbow and brown trout, which come not only for the foods being washed in but also for the somewhat warmer water carried by these brooks.

Angler access to Cayuga Lake is excellent. Public facilities are distributed all around the lake and private marinas assist in supplemental access and in providing angler support services. Major population centers and the associated non-angling services are found in Ithaca and Seneca Falls.

Allen H. Treman State Marine Park on the Cayuga Inlet in Ithaca, off Route 89, is the largest launch facility on the lake. You must navigate the canal for a short distance before passing the lighthouse that guards the southern port. Pay attention to this area as off-channel waters represent both a boating danger and a fishing opportunity in the early spring for browns and landlocked salmon. This area of the lake has the largest early

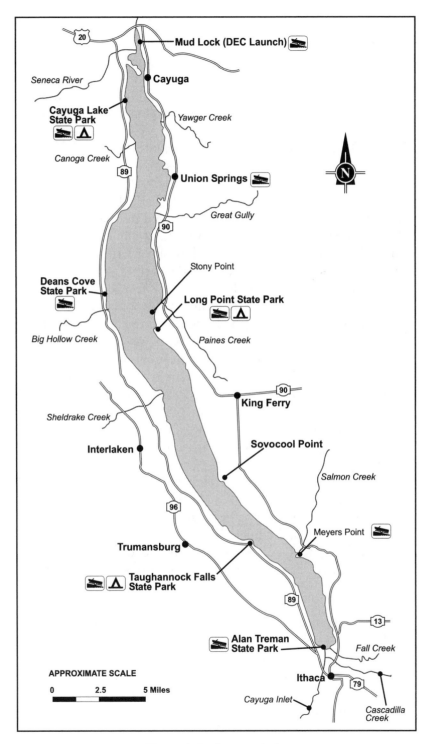

Figure 2.1 Cayuga Lake

mass of warm water during the spring, and it attracts these game fish by the thousands. Flat line trolling with stick baits such as the Rapala will normally provide you with plenty of action. Don't be surprised if you hook into an out-of-season northern pike of 10 or more pounds as well.

Seven miles north of Ithaca on Route 89 along the west shore of the lake, is Taughannock State Park. There is a small marina and double launch that is bubbled during the winter for year-round access to open water. Launching, however, is limited to boats with a relatively low super-structure in that you must navigate under a foot bridge before you reach the lake. The height of the bridge is 6½ to 7 feet, depending on the water level of the lake. Boats in the 20-foot class will often drop their canvas just to use the facility because of its proximity to some of the best angling on the lake.

At mid-lake, in the township of Romulus on Route 89, is Deans Cove. It is the newest access site to the lake. Traveling north, the next public launch is at Cayuga Lake State Park off Route 89 on the Lower Lake Road in Seneca Falls. This facility gives you direct access to some of the best bass fishing in the state. Cayuga Lake State Park and The Cove, a private marina just south of the park, play host to the majority of the 50-plus bass fishing tournaments held each season on Cayuga Lake.

Some of the largest professional bass tournaments held in the state are now scheduled for Cayuga Lake. Red Man, the New York State B.A.S.S. Federation and others are often scheduled two seasons in advance to assure they have facilities to conduct their contests that are now attracting upwards of 200 anglers. Bass events are so popular you can fish a bass tournament nearly every weekend and never leave Cayuga Lake.

The average tournament bass is 1½ pounds, but the winner with a 5-bass live well will seldom have less than 15 pounds of bass, and more often than not, the total may approach or break 20 pounds.

THE FINGER LAKES AT A GLANCE

	Cayuga	Seneca	Keuka	Canandaigua	Skaneateles	Owasco	Conesus	Otisco	Hemlock	Honeoye	Canadice
Area (square miles)	66.87	66.61	18.30	16.57	13.60	10.60	4.97	3.46	3.23	2.71	1.05
Principal Game Fish	LT, BT, RT, LS, LB, SB, NP, CP	LT, BT, RT, LS, LB, SB, NP	LT, BT, RT, LS, SB, NP	LT, BT, RT, SB, CP	LT, BT, RT, LS, SB	LT, BT, RT, LB, SB, NP	WP, NP, LB, CP	WP, TM, SB, BT, LB	LT, LS, RT, BT, SB, CP	LB, WP, CP	LT, BT, RT, CP, SB
Maximum Depth (feet)	435	618	185	278	300	180	66	76/15*	91	30	83
Average Depth (feet)	181	291	102	129	145	97	38	34/6*	45	16	54
Shoreline (miles)	84.8	75.4	58.4	35.9	32.8	24.7	18.5	13.4	17.1	10.8	7.1
Mean Thermal Stratification (feet)**	37	38	33	49	35	37	39	40	28	Does not stratify	25
Number of Public Motorboat Launches	8	6	2	4	2	1	2	0	1	1	1
Number of Public Cartop/Canoe Launches	0	1	0	0	1	0	1	1	1	1	0

*   Otisco Lake has two basins.

**   Depth at which the thermocline is normally found, averaged over the months during which stratification occurs.

Species Key:

BT	= Brown Trout	NP	= Northern Pike
CP	= Chain Pickerel	RT	= Rainbow Trout
LB	= Largemouth Bass	SB	= Smallmouth Bass
LS	= Landlocked Salmon	TM	= Tiger Muskie
LT	= Lake Trout	WP	= Walleyed Pike

The majority of this bass action will be in the northern six miles of the lake, but winning stringers of bass have come from as far south as Farleys Point and Frontenac Island on the east side and East Varick on the west side. The quality of bass fishing in the northern weed beds of the lake has actually been improved in recent years, largely because of the use of mechanical weed harvesters that not only allow easier boat access but also open more fishing water.

The deep water navigation channel that begins at the twin buoys opposite Canoga and runs to Mud Lock at the beginning of the barge canal is another favorite location for big bass in the heat of summer. Ice fishing along this same channel has, in past years, produced bass in excess of five pounds. However, a change in the fishing regulations now has the bass fishing in both Cayuga and Skaneateles Lake closed on November 30. The same area is still a popular location for perch and northern pike through the ice.

The catch-and-release bass tournaments do not seem to have affected the quality of bass fishing in Cayuga Lake. DEC's radio transmitter research on the location of release of these tournament fish suggests that deep water release is better than a release at the scale site. But, the total weight and number of bass caught has not diminished over the years while tournament pressure has increased perhaps tenfold.

The northernmost launch on Cayuga Lake is a DEC facility at Mud Lock. This is located off Route 90, and is most suitable for small trailerable boats and cartops. It gives you immediate access to semi-sheltered waters and quality bass fishing.

Union Springs on Route 90 operates a municipal launch at Frontenac Park that will handle boats up to 25 feet. This facility is free and has parking for 30 cars and trailers.

Long Point State Park, at mid-lake on the east side off Route 90, is located at the northern edge of the best cold water fishing on the lake. It is on a leg of what I call the northern horseshoe trolling pattern that circles a bowl of deep water. This is a favorite rainbow trout area in the fall of the year.

The Town of Lansing operates the Myers Point launch off Route 34B approximately five miles north of Ithaca on the west side of the lake.

Both Long Point and Myers Point, at the mouth of Salmon Creek, offer good shore fishing for trout and salmon in the cold water months of the year. Taughannock Point on the west side has the most consistent and best cold weather shore fishing on the lake. Its abrupt drop-offs allow anglers to reach depths of 70 feet by casting from shore. Taughannock is also the area where lighted bobber fishing at night began in the Finger Lakes.

It's also where Peter Slack of Sheldrake set a line-class landlocked salmon record for the Freshwater Fishing Hall of Fame with a trophy of 10 pounds, 9 ounces on six pound test line. He caught the trophy fishing a golden shiner five feet under a bobber and using a noodle rod. Brown trout and lake trout exceeding 10 pounds are frequent trophies of this exceptional shore fishing area. Smallmouth bass are also likely trophies along this shore. Fish tight to the bank during the summer months.

Cayuga Lake State Park offers some excellent shore fishing for crappie in the spring of the year, but for even better opportunity, energetic anglers will hike out along the railroad dike that crosses the north end of the lake. Fathead minnows lip hooked on gold-plated bait hooks and small jigs fished under a bobber seem to be the preferred methods.

In the central and southern deep water areas of the lake open water fishing never stops, even during the winter months. But knowledgeable anglers target mid-March to begin their search for trophy sized landlocked salmon. In 2001 the average landlocked salmon weighed 3.8 pounds and measured 20 plus inches. The average lake trout was similar in size while brown and rainbow trout averaged a pound less. This is the time when the salmon are concentrated in the warm water discharges from the local tributaries such as the Cayuga Inlet, Salmon or Taughannock Creeks. And don't hesitate to work off the no-name tributaries after a warm rain has triggered the

Northern pike are not as common as most other gamefish in the Finger Lakes, but these good battlers are always a possibility in Cayuga Lake. This early season trophy was caught while the anglers trolled shallow water for trout and salmon.

seasonal flows.

A surface temperature gauge will help trollers find productive water, but you can almost fish by sight. If there is a mud line – one often forms at the southernmost portion of the lake – work it. Flat line troll with long lines and terminal baits such as small spoons, vibrating lures such as Fire Plugs and Hot Shots, or stickbaits including AC Shiners and Rapalas.

Light line angling seems to result in more strikes than more traditional line weights. Captain Bill Haessner specializes in four pound test and 12 foot noodle rods, and enjoys a great deal of success in the first month of early spring angling. He readily admits that his methods may not be for everyone, but says an angler will take a lot more fish with six or eight pound test line than he will with 10 or 12. Haessner uses a lot of hot colors in his fishing. Chartreuse and flame reds are his favorites.

On any day you have a chance of taking a mixed creel of all the available salmonids. Lake trout will usually outnumber all others by at least four to one, even when surface trolling in early spring. If you are lucky you will connect with one of the leaping, heart-stopping landlocks with every fifth fish.

In the fall of the year, landlocks will again be vulnerable as they and brown trout stage off these same streams before making their spawning runs. While natural spawning is not very successful, it does not stop these fish from trying.

In the fall of the year my favorite fishing method is trolling with downriggers off Taughannock Point. Small spoons such as the Alpena Diamond or the small Stinger series, spoons less than two inches long, have produced some dramatic results. I like to fish at the height of the autumn color, and troll not more than 100 yards off shore, working back and forth across the stream mouth. My lures are normally set approximately 30 feet below the surface, and I will use a stacked "cheater leader" five to ten feet above my main line. The added leader is attached to the main line with a snap swivel but held in place on the downrigger cable by a rubber band or a special stacking release. The spoons will all be of similar design and color to imitate a school effect in the presentation.

Often the extra lures are not necessary, and if you can fish without them, do it. Even with clean lines you can still get into some delightful fire drills. I have had four landlocked salmon on at the same time on three different occasions fishing off Taughannock in the fall of the year. I have yet to land more than two. Whenever you have more than one salmon on at the same time, they seem to have a way of teaming up to wrap lines around downrigger cables, attach spoons to your weights and in general make a fool of even the most experienced angler.

When the leaves are totally off the trees you may have to fish north, off the Milliken Station, now known as Sovocool, to have the same fast action. Trout and salmon gather there, attracted by the warm water as the days grow shorter. Shore fishing off the power plant is available but limited because of the parking problems. Follow the signs off Route 90 and Starks Road carefully. Parking in a no parking zone will normally result in your vehicle being towed from the area.

Lake trout is the bread and butter fish of Cayuga Lake. They are the most common angler fare, and can sometimes be picked up almost at will. Summer deep water trolling patterns for lake trout on Cayuga Lake will often be north and south. But running the triangulation pattern of Myers, Taughannock and Milliken, or Sheldrake, Long Point and Milliken is as traditional as the use of silver plated spoons. If the thermocline is established, lake trout will usually be found in or just below it. Browns, rainbows and salmon will usually be above the thermocline, sometimes as shallow as 40 feet below the surface.

Anglers concentrating on lake trout should search with the slowest trolling speeds possible, about two miles per hour. If your target is salmon or the other species of trout increase your trolling speed to 2.5 to 3 mph. The most critical factor, however, is to match your trolling speed to the optimal action of the lure or bait that you are using. Judging the best speed requires that you run the lure next to the boat and adjust your speed for the best action before setting a downrigger or thermocline rig.

Still-fishing from anchored deep water spots does not have the following on Cayuga Lake that it has on Seneca. But on Cayuga Lake, bait fishing for trout from shore is more popular. Local residents will often row a small boat out to set their bait rig in deep water and then return to the dock where they can enjoy a leisurely wait.

Smallmouth bass and perch are almost totally ignored in the southern waters of Cayuga Lake. Casting jigs tight to the

Jumbo panfish are very effective at inducting new recruits into the sport of angling.

steep ledges along the shores can produce plenty of action with both species. In most cases, this is ideal habitat. If you don't catch fish, move in closer. Many places in the lower half of the lake require that your bait land within inches of the shore.

Cayuga Lake may be one of the best destinations in the Finger Lakes. Anglers wanting to make this water a vacation experience can easily headquarter themselves at any one of the three state parks, Cayuga, Long Point or Taughannock. Both Taughannock and Cayuga have cabins and all three have camp-sites. With more than 60 square miles of water you will never run out of new places to fish.

CHAPTER 3
KEUKA LAKE
by C. Scott Sampson

B y today's standards Seth Green, considered to be the father of American fish culture, might be called a fish hog. Keuka Lake was his favorite water and he knew just how to reap the bounty that was held in the blue depths and sheltered by the steep hillsides.

"On August 28 last I took, with hook and line, 19 salmon trout (lake trout) weighing 113 pounds, and on October 1, 1880, 33 black bass weighing 106 pounds," wrote Green. He also said that it was his opinion Keuka Lake was unsurpassed by any water in America as a fishing resort.

The one-time U.S. Fish Commissioner was not bragging about his catch as much as he was just stating facts. Weight and numbers were important to Green. He was a commercial angler who worked the Finger Lakes and then sold his catch in Rochester.

It was at Keuka Landing, opposite Bluff Point on the eastern shore and a short row from some of the best deep water angling in the lake, that Green developed his multi-leader fishing system that is still used by many anglers today. The Seth Green or thermocline rig was, and still is, largely a "meat-pole" rig allowing anglers to work the waters from the surface to depths of 100 feet or more at the same time. Today the linen line has been replaced with a steel main line and monofilament leaders, but the initial design remains the same.

A heavy lead weight of up to three pounds took the main line to the bottom. Running off the main line were leaders, normally 20 feet long and spaced 25 feet apart so that, if the line went straight for any reason (including the angler stopping to fight a fish) the baits or lures would not become tangled. While the leaders were set 25 feet apart, when using the rig the lures actually were closer together as the main line entered the water at an angle and stayed that way as Green and his followers rowed up and down the lake. The early standard for the number of leaders was seven. That, in later days, went to five leaders when anglers were limited to 15 hook points or one treble hook per leader. With the popularity of single hooked spoons and the strength of steel line, anglers began exploring the depths with as many as 15 leaders on a single main line. Regualtions now limit the multi-leaders to five per main line.

Setting a Seth Green rig and retrieving it, even in modern times, is work. The system utilizes a large saltwater reel mounted on a very stiff boat rod. The rod is equipped with large roller guides to not only handle the steel line but also the swivels, "C" shaped clevis, or double steel beads that are crimped in place to make the leader attachments. Each of the leaders are very carefully coiled by hand either into a sectioned box made just for them or on plastic leader spools. Either way, if you are playing a good trout, the last twenty feet is hand to hand combat.

Charlie Jensen, a local expert on the advancement of the Seth Green rig and its evolution to steel line, has been working with a narrow coil spring spinner shaft to attach his leaders. The link is opened by sliding the spring back, and the leader can be quickly reattached to a line on a large-eyed spinning rod. Jensen feels the results are more satisfying, and he loses fewer fish at the boat. However, you must be careful not to exceed the two-lines-per-angler law.

Keuka Lake is the third largest of the Finger Lakes. It has 18.3 square miles of surface, roughly one-third that of either Seneca or Cayuga Lake, but, its "Y" shape configuration pro-

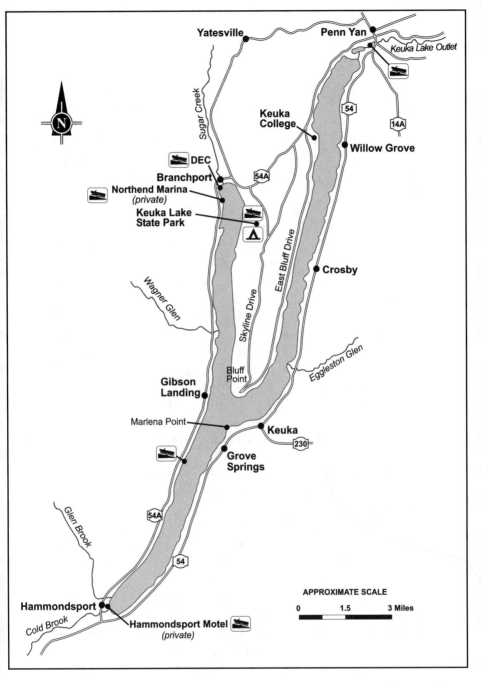

Figure 3.1   Keuka Lake

vides nearly as many miles of shoreline: 58.4. Keuka's overall length is just over 22 miles as measured from Penn Yan to Hammondsport. The lake has an average depth of 101 feet, with a maximum depth of 185 feet. It is fed by Cold Brook on the south and Sugar (or Guyanoga) Creek at Branchport. Its only outlet is at Penn Yan and that flows into Seneca Lake six miles to the east.

Keuka is principally a cold water lake, with natural spawning lake trout the main target species. It has the third largest lake trout harvest of any inland water in the state, trailing only Seneca and Cayuga Lakes for total pounds produced.

The steep-sided ledges along the shoreline make for ideal smallmouth bass and perch habitat. Smallmouth bass attract nearly as many anglers to the lake as do the trout. Less than 10 percent of Keuka is suitable for largemouth bass, northern pike and pickerel. Fishing for these species is generally limited to the southern and northern tips of the lake.

The lake is not only deep, it also has exceptionally clear water. With more than 25 percent of its 187 square miles of watershed in forest, it remains one of the jewels of the Finger Lakes. The quality of the lake combined with its proximity to the population centers of Rochester and Elmira-Corning also makes Keuka one of the more popular recreational waters.

Keuka was a popular bass fishing tournament site in years past, a fact that may have influenced the enactment of a 45 mile per hour speed limit law for daylight hours and a 25 mph limit from ½ hour after sunset to ½ hour before sunrise. The same law requires boaters to reduce speed to 5 mph within 200 yards of shore or any anchored boat.

If you get the idea Keuka Lake can become crowded on summer weekends, you are correct. But, there seems to be an excellent unofficial exchange of activities. Anglers have the early morning hours and evenings while water skiers and other recreational boaters seem to take over between 11 a.m. and 4 p.m.

This unofficial and unregulated zoning is an important part of the Keuka culture because of limited access to the lake. Penn

Yan has a four-ramp launch at the village park located off Route 14A on Water Street. These ramps are on the north side of the Keuka Outlet and you must travel a short distance in the canal and past the former Penn Yan Boat Company before gaining access to the lake. Off Route 54A, at the Branchport tip of the lake, is Keuka Lake State Park. This facility offers direct access to the lake as well as 150 non-electric campsites for those wishing to spend several days or even weeks learning the water.

The DEC has finished a long legal process for gaining a public access site at Hammondsport but has not been able to fund it. As such the Hammondsport Motel may be the best private facility for access to the southern waters. It can handle boats up to 22 feet. While there are marinas that service the lake, they are inclined to reserve parking and launch facilities for their regular customers. The Town of Wayne has a gravel site off Route 54 and Urbana has a site off 54A but these are reserved for residents only.

Keuka has a significant angling history. Lake trout are native to the water and reproduce here naturally. Even today with the modern angling technology and superior catch rates of less than two hours to catch a legal salmonid, lake trout still maintain themselves through natural procreation.

Lake trout stocking for many years supplemented the natural reproduction. But in the late '60s anglers saw a decline in the size of lake trout indicating there was an overpopulation. They were too abundant for the forage base. Stocking was stopped for lake trout and started for alewives between 1968 and 1971, and the situation was corrected.

Today, an angler can expect lake trout to average $3\frac{1}{2}$ pounds. Brown trout will average three pounds and rainbows under three pounds. Landlocked salmon will generally range from two to nearly four pounds, depending on the year class or classes that are dominant in a given season.

However, like many of the other Finger Lakes, trophy specimens of all species do occur. Each year, Keuka can be expected to give up a few salmonids that exceed 10 pounds. A lake trout

of 14 or even 15 pounds could also be expected.

Alewives have been part of the lake's forage base since the 1860s. Smelt, whose introduction here is a mystery, have been a part of the fishery since the mid-1960s.

A California strain of steelhead was introduced to the lake in 1897 at Cold Brook. It is thought that this strain still largely represents the resident rainbows that continue to spawn successfully in both Cold Brook and Sugar Creeks. In 1946, an early state record rainbow trout was caught in the area of Hammondsport. It weighed 21 pounds. Despite that early success, what had been a self-sustaining rainbow fishery is now being supplemented with annual stocking of wild Finger Lakes strain yearlings.

Brown trout were initially not stocked in Keuka Lake, but at least a few escapees entered the lake from the state hatchery located on the headwaters of Cold Brook. These immigrants were to later become famous, producing two state records.

In June 1979, a 22 pound, 4 ounce trophy was caught by Carson Fitzwater in the southern area of the lake. That record lasted until February 1983 when Bruce Davis, while fishing open water off Cold Brook with a jig, caught a brown weighing 23 pounds, 12 ounces and measuring 35¾ inches.

Two years previous, Davis had caught a 17 pound brown using the same method. He and his fishing partner, Rick Stratton, had consistently caught browns and landlocked salmon in the four and five pound class by casting their ⅛ ounce synthetic-hair brown and white jigs toward shore and then working them back toward the 30 foot water where their 12 foot open utility boat was anchored.

Lake Ontario has now claimed the state's brown trout record several times over. But, by any standard these Keuka browns were impressive fish.

Keuka Lake has no sea lamprey because the barrier dams on Keuka Outlet prevent their egress from Seneca Lake. The absence of this parasitic fish is one of the reasons many Keuka fish have been able to achieve trophy status.

Since 1980, Keuka Lake has received an annual stocking of brown trout. Browns are now an important part of the fishery here, and they capture the attention of anglers on a year-round basis.

Landlocked salmon are also relatively new to the lake, having been stocked only since 1976, and they are serving to further diversify Keuka's cold water fishery. These fish are highly prized, but remain unpredictable and therefore take second place to the bread and butter lake trout.

The lake trout is the most eagerly sought fish and by far the most numerous species to be found in the angler's creel. Year in and year out, for every 16 salmonids taken 15 are lake trout.

Keuka anglers also enjoy productive night fishing for lake trout. While less popular today than in years past, night angling is still practiced in every area of the lake, but most frequently in the waters off Bluff Point.

A boat is anchored in 100 or more feet of water. A battery powered 25-watt electric light is suspended over the side to attract baitfish. The light may be a floating waterproof model but is often made of household components including a large reflector to concentrate the light in the water and keep it out of the angler's eyes. In the old days lanterns were used to attract the bait fish.

When the light has done its job of attracting baitfish, the angler lowers a multi-hooked line straight down 50 to 70 feet. Live smelt or sawbellies are hooked just below the dorsal fin and allowed to swim free with the natural bait that is attracted to the light.

Trout fishing on Keuka Lake is available in nearly every deep water location. On the Penn Yan arm, it starts approximately at Willow Grove and runs south to the flats off Hammondsport. On the Branchport arm of the lake, trout fishing begins at the state park and continues south.

The area between Marlena Point and Bluff Point has a major concentration of lake trout. Bait and artificial lures seem to work equally well. The traditional Sutton spoons, made in

A sport fisherman with a legal mixed bag of perch, bass and trout. The Finger Lakes offer both diversity and quality. Note that on some of these lakes certain species can legally be sold.

Naples, are the most common artificial lure. The spoons might be worked off a Seth Green rig or even straight copper wire to get the lure on or near the bottom.

Once the lake stratifies in the summer and the thermocline is established, the downrigger will outfish most other methods. The controlled depth trolling device allows you to place the lure at the exact level where the fish are. Lake trout generally like slow trolling speeds, and you might try a vibrating lure such as the Fire Plug or FlatFish to wake them up and entice them to strike. The Peanut Plug is another excellent choice.

The most active areas for brown and rainbow trout are off Hammondsport and Cold Brook. But both these species, as well as landlocked salmon, will seek out any warm water in the cooler months of the year. In the fall, work off creek mouths where warm water flows occur, as well as the area of the Keuka Outlet. Also consider the hydro-power discharge at the Kendall Point power plant opposite Bluff Point on the east side of the lake. Live bait drifted under bobbers is a common method for taking these surface cruising fish.

Smallmouth bass are king of the warm water species on the lake. They are most readily available from the opening of the season on the third Saturday in June until mid-July. Most anglers will concentrate their efforts on casting crankbaits or jigs in relatively shallow water off the rock rubble points in the lake. These include Willow Grove, Keuka College, Bluff, Eggleston and Marlena Points. In the southern arm of the lake, Urbana, Two Mile and Willow Points are good starting locations.

Much of the smallmouth bass fishing by visiting anglers will be done with deep running crankbaits or jigs. Local anglers will more often drift with softshell crabs or crayfish. Either method can produce an average smallmouth of 2½ pounds. Deep water winter angling, especially off Bluff Point, has consistently produced bass in the range of four pounds, and some have exceeded six pounds. There is also limited ice fishing, primarily in the northern portions of the lake. This is a perch fishery for the most part, but smallmouth and largemouth bass, pickerel and northern pike are also possible.

In mid-July the smallmouth go deep, and often suspend above the thermocline. They appear to follow the bait schools, and will often be taken 50 feet deep by anglers. These smallmouth are often caught incidental to trout and salmon by anglers fishing traditional salmonid spoons. It is not unusual to have a mixed creel. In the fall and winter months the smallmouth become structure oriented again. Anglers should once again concentrate their efforts on the ledges and rock rubble slopes off the points and shorelines where there is an immediate drop-off.

Jigs tipped with plastic Mr. Twister bodies will allow you to work the 20 to 30 foot depths necessary in all but the early season. Deer hair home-tied jigs are also used quite frequently because of the large number of rigs lost in this type of rock rubble bottom fishing, and because you have to fish with relatively light line. Small diameter line is a requirement in the clear water, and it's also necessary in order to feel the fish strike in deep water. The norm is six to ten pound test, never more. The bait or lure is most often tied directly to the line.

Yellow perch inhabit the same general areas as the smallmouth bass, and are second only to the smallmouth as an important warm water fish. Drifting with minnows or jigs is the standard angling method. You should expect to catch 10 and 12 inch perch. If they are small, move so you can connect with a school of larger fish.

Largemouth bass are limited to the shallow areas near Penn Yan and Branchport. They also share these weed filled areas with northern pike and pickerel, but all three species are secondary to other angling opportunities. Traditional spinner baits, plastic worms and even top water plugs can bring action.

Panfish are abundant in Keuka Lake. Rock bass and crappie as large as one pound are possible. Good fishing for brown bullhead is limited to the spring of the year; these fish are usually caught in the mud stained wash of the tributaries.

Chapter 4
CANANDAIGUA LAKE
by C. Scott Sampson

Alarge white-painted rock sits on the southeast corner shore line of Canandaigua Lake. It acts as a landmark and, more importantly, identifies the eastern edge of the bar that runs across the southern end of the lake.

Anglers have painted the rock white since before the turn of the century. It took the place of a point of land or other identifying characteristic totally absent at that location. In the early days, finding a special spot was almost a science and critical to success. There were no electronic depth finders, and often no motors. Anglers needed the land based guides and used informal triangulation to identify their special spots.

The bar the white rock marks has a sudden drop-off to deep water that is just as important today as it was at the turn of the century. Its structure attracts the fish. The bar runs nearly straight across the lake from the white rock to Coy(es) Point, just north of Woodville. The drop is abrupt; from depths of less than a dozen feet, it dives to over 100.

The white rock is also the landmark that, when aligned with Cooks Point, can help you find "The Mounds". These are two underwater hills nearly 60 yards wide and 50 feet high. They are the only structure in a relatively smooth lake bottom in 150 feet of water. It is an important holding area for big trout.

When Canandaigua Lake had a significant walleye population the bar was one of the favorite fishing locations. It was also the prime location for whitefish and cisco, two other once-abundant species. Today, it is a prime lake trout location, and in the spring and fall a location where rainbows stage before running Naples Creek. Brown trout will work the top of the bar seeking the warmest possible water in both the spring and the fall.

Walleye, according to early literature, were quite abundant in the era of 1924. Two and three-pound fish were common. In 10 years they were averaging five and six pounds, but were less common. The last major walleye catches occurred in the mid-forties. While I know of no recent catches, DEC reports them as rare.

The collapse of the walleye fishing may be blamed on the introduction of smelt in 1924. These baitfish-turned-predator established themselves by dining on walleye fry. The balance of cisco was also knocked askew, which effected the overall size of the lake trout. But, with the establishment of the alewife as a major forage base in the 1950s, there has been a substantial improvement in the lake trout fishing.

Canandaigua Lake, because of its proximity to Rochester, receives some of the highest fishing pressure of any of the Finger Lakes. Angler trips per acre of water is nearly four times what is experienced on Seneca and Cayuga Lakes. Recreational boating activities, including wind surfing, are also popular. If you can schedule your fishing, weekdays are more productive, especially in the northern waters. Canandaigua's 36-mile shoreline is quite populated, with 83 percent in residential or commercial use and only 12 percent in forest or agriculture.

Public access on Canandaigua Lake is better than many Finger Lakes, but is still inadequate considering the boating and angling pressure. There are two major launch sites. The Canandaigua Marine Park, just off Routes 5 and 20 at the mouth of Sucker Brook, has parking for 110 cars and trailers as well as pump out facilities. The site at Woodville on Route 21, three miles north of Naples, used to be a cartop facility only. But it has been expanded to hard ramps and there is parking for 80

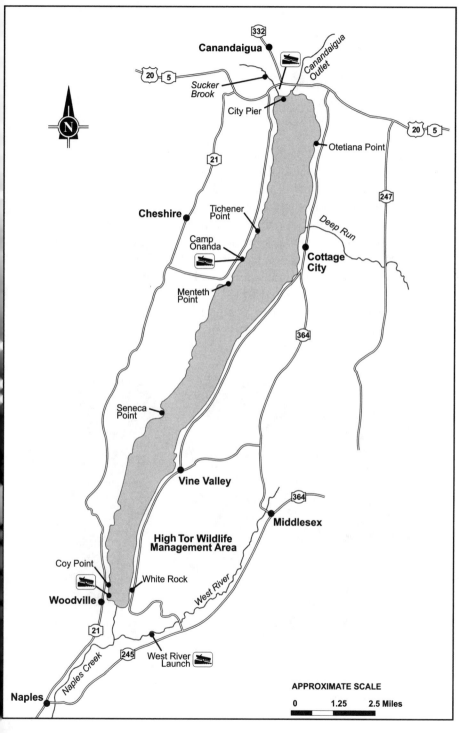

Figure 4.1   Canandaigua Lake

vehicles and trailers.

A third launch site, on the West River off Route 245 six miles south of Middlesex, is very limited. It is more often used by largemouth bass anglers intent on fishing the river, or by hunters in the fall of the year. West River is also a choice area for bullhead and black crappie. While it is possible to reach the lake from this launch it may be advisable to use the Woodville facility so you don't waste your fishing time in very slow travel.

A fourth launch, open only in the winter months, has been built at Camp Onanda, a former YWCA facility. It is six miles south of Canandaigua on County Road 16 (West Lake Road). The seven-acre shoreline belongs to DEC while the remaining 73 acres has been deeded to the City of Canandaigua. In the summer, the facility is run as a park by the city. A user fee is charged during daytime hours. In the non-summer months, the facility is a fishing access site that includes a hard-surface

The main boat access to Canandaigua Lake is in the city of Canandaigua at the north end of the lake on the narrow and shallow channel called Sucker Brook.

launch ramp. It will provide open water access to the lake in the winter months when the north and south ends are frozen closed. This facility also offers some of the best shore angling for trout available on the lake. The drop-off is fast enough that trout can be caught from shore even during the summer months, and it's a prime location for winter shore angling. Shore angling access can also be found on the east side of the lake at a small county park at Deep Run and at the City Pier in Canandaigua.

Canandaigua is the fourth largest of the Finger Lakes. With its 16.57 square miles of surface, 15.8 mile length, average depth of 129 feet and maximum depth of 278 feet, it is primarily a cold water lake. The lake trout is by far the most abundant and popular game fish available. Lake trout angling is almost totally dependent on annual stocking. Stocking levels are currently 12,400 spring yearlings and 24,100 fall fingerlings.

Rainbow trout, originally introduced to the lake before the turn of the century, are now totally self-sustaining with natural reproduction from Naples Creek, the lake's only major tributary. Brown trout are stocked at a rate of approximately 8,000 yearlings annually. Landlocked salmon stocking in the '50s was a failure.

A substantial smallmouth bass fishery is also an important part of Canandaigua Lake. Three-pound bass are common and a six-pound smallmouth is possible. Largemouth bass, perch, pickerel and northern pike are all of secondary importance, and generally limited to the northern and southern tips of the lake.

Canandaigua's lake trout fishery is unique in that it takes seven to eight years for a lake trout to reach 20 inches. That is nearly three years more than in most of the other Finger Lakes. Once they reach that stage, their growth takes off, and the production is comparable to growth rates in other lakes. The average lake trout caught are 20 to 21 inches and weigh 3 to 3½ pounds. A lake trout of 26 pounds was reported to have been caught in 1962, and each year trout of 15 pounds are recorded.

The largest rainbow trout are caught in Naples Creek during the spawning run in April. A 10 pound fish is common, but the average for the lake is three pounds and 18 inches. Anglers have never been able to identify a location or a method for consistently taking the big rainbow trout that are known to exist in this lake.

Brown trout up to 10 pounds are caught in Cananadaigua Lake, but the average is just under three pounds. These fish are temperature oriented, and are most susceptible in the spring and fall when they congregate in the warm water flumes of the tributaries. In the fall they tend to concentrate at the two outlet dams at the north end of the lake. The two outlets combine into one before they leave the city limits, and the Canandaigua Lake Outlet eventually flows into the Barge Canal at Lyons.

Despite the fishing pressure on the lake, the overall catch rate for salmonids has remained at just over two hours of fishing effort to catch a legal trout. It's a very acceptable success rate as judged by angler satisfaction and fisheries management standards.

While I mentioned the southern portion of the lake for trout fishing, it is far from the only area. Most points seem to attract and hold trout populations. Tichenor, Menteth, Black and Seneca on the west side and Cottage City Bay, Long and Whiskey Points on the east side are good locations. In the spring and fall of the year lake trout are often on the rock rubble off these points at depths of about 40 feet. In the spring, still fishing with live smelt or alewives is most successful. As the waters warm the trout move deeper. Once the thermocline is established they will suspend in or just below it with little regard for structure. At this time the Hemlock Spinner, an attractor with a live bait harness, is the standard rig.

Night fishing for lake trout is also popular on Canandaigua, but there are a number of changes from the method used on Keuka Lake. The Canandaigua angler anchors in 100 to 140 feet of water and wants the boat perfectly still. By putting out anchors at the bow and stern there will be no swing. They use

An aerial photograph of the beautiful Canandaigua Lake.
(Courtesy DEC)

the light over the side, but usually only to attract and net the sawbellies attracted to it. In the old days they used dynamite caps to stun the bait (strictly illegal now). Modern day anglers will often buy sawbellies or smelt rather than take the time to gather their own.

The bait rigs for night fishing consist of five short leaders, only 30 to 40 inches long and separated on the main line by 10 feet so a 50 foot range of water is worked. The line is lowered over the side and stopped at 70 to 90 feet.

Most night fishing on Canandaigua begins at midnight, and if you do not have your limit by first light you can change to trolling methods.

Throughout the Finger Lakes many trollers are turning away from the heavy thermocline rigs in favor of lighter rods and downrigger techniques. The advantages of the multi-lure presentation can be duplicated with the use of additional leaders used on your downrigger system.

"Cheater" leaders can increase your chances of catching trout. The name suggests there is something illegal about the system but that is not at all true. The extra leaders are considered a part of your main line just as they are with the Seth Green system. Under conventional downrigging, the norm is one system-one lure. But I like to add a cheater leader in a fixed position five to 10 feet above the bomb. The cheater is a length of monofilament line, normally six feet long, with a snap-swivel on each end. Your second lure is attached to one end and the other snap circles the main line. The cheater is positioned above the bomb by looping a light rubber band around the downrigger cable. It is then passed through itself and pulled snug. The open loop of the band is hooked into the same snap that went around the main line. There are a number of commercial stacking releases that can take the place of the rubber band, but for a cheater this method is inexpensive and effective.

I like to pre-condition my release rubber bands by leaving them in the sun to lessen their strength.

A fish striking the main line lure will also release the cheater, and it is then played in the normal light-tackle manner. If the fish strikes the cheater, the rubber band will break first and then the leader slides toward the bomb releasing the main line as well. The leader continues to slide to the end of the line but is stopped by the main-line lure. You play the fish in normal fashion but in landing it, be careful not to catch the net bag with the main lure. The leader, at this time, is an extension of the main line. Because of this, it must be relatively short so you can continue to use the rod to guide the fish to the net.

You can add up to four cheater leaders so long as you do not exceed the five lure and 15-hook-point New York State limit for your main line. I normally use only one fixed cheater. I like to run similar spoons on the main line as well as the cheater. If I have different sizes of the same spoon that are speed compatible, I will place the smaller spoon on the short leader so it looks as though a larger fish might be chasing a smaller fish.

If fishing action is really slow, I run a second cheater that is free moving. The sliding cheater is hooked around the main line after the downrigger and fixed cheater are set. The sliding leader, with a light flutter spoon, will sink to a point about mid-way between the fixed cheater and the surface of the water. It will hold at the farthest point of the curve in the bow of the main line.

You now have effective coverage at three levels. If the bomb is set for 90 feet, you have a lure at that level, the fixed cheater at 80 feet and the sliding cheater at 40.

In Canandaigua Lake and most of the deep water Finger Lakes you are targeting lake trout on the lower baits and perhaps a brown, rainbow or landlocked salmon on the slider. The critical issue when fishing multiple lures is to have them speed compatible. That is to say, the lures must produce their maximum fish catching action at the same trolling speed.

Smallmouth bass are distributed throughout the lake, but are especially attracted to the deep drop-offs strewn with rock and rubble. That is nearly any place off the east or west sides of the lake and in the area of Squaw Island on the north end. The areas of White Rock, Long Point, Vine Valley, Deep Run and Otetiana Point on the east side are excellent locations to start your fishing. On the west side, Long, Seneca, Black and Tichenor Points and the Pump House are good choices.

Jigs and deep running crankbaits should catch early season smallmouth. Work the baits close to shore for best results. As the fish move deeper you might change to jigging spoons as a means of getting deep quickly. Len Lisenbee's favorite system for smallmouth is to use a three-way swivel with a drop sinker on one connect and a Rapala on an 18-inch leader on the other.

He adjusts his sinker weight for the depth he desires to drift or troll and bounces the weight on the bottom whenever possible.

Smallmouth bass on Canandaigua Lake suspend over the thermocline during the summer in a manner similar to those fish in Keuka Lake. They are caught incidentally by anglers fishing for brown and rainbow trout.

Most anglers will ignore the suspended bass. They will instead fish crayfish or minnows on bottom, working them along the points and fishing progressively deeper and deeper until they find fish.

Perch will often be caught while fishing for smallmouth, but don't overlook schooled perch in the spring and fall of the year when they are in the weed beds at the northern and southern ends of the lake. These areas will also produce largemouth bass and, at the southern end, pickerel.

Chapter 5
SKANEATELES LAKE
by C. Scott Sampson

You notice it the second you turn onto the half-mile drive off Route 41A that leads to the DEC boat launch site on Skaneateles Lake. The drive is lined with wooden posts and no parking signs. The signs are overkill - there is no room to pull off the road. A postage-stamp-sized parking area, with room for about 30 cars and trailers, overlooks the sparkling waters of what is one of the most protected of the Finger Lakes. It is obvious there is a desire to limit the number of boats on the lake.

Aluminum floating docks, held in place with U-shaped pipes anchored in cement seawalls, frame the double ramp. The floating docks are necessary to maintain a reasonable height to the water with the rise and fall of the lake's level, which can be as much as 16 feet. The City of Syracuse draws off water at rates in excess of 50 million gallons a day. During the drought of 1987 the lake level dropped drastically and remained low, leaving cottage owners and marinas high and dry. It was not until the flood-like rains from Hurricane Hugo in 1989 that the lake returned to normal levels.

Being a giant water supply has it advantages. The watershed has numerous anti-pollution control regulations to prevent any alterations in building or land use which might decrease the water quality.

Skaneateles Lake has a transparent quality. You can look through 20 feet of water and see objects as though they were

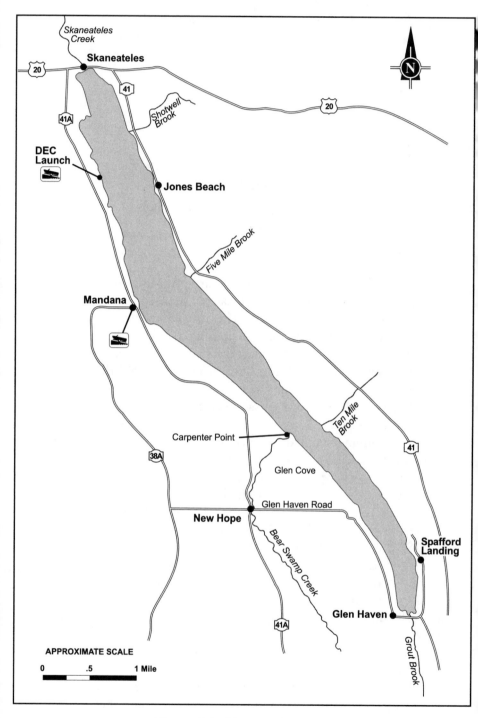

Figure 5.1   Skaneateles Lake

just under the surface. That makes fishing more exciting and more difficult as the fish tend to shy away from the boat and the landing net.

The lake is relatively deep, with a mean depth of 145 feet and a maximum depth of 300 feet. Its overall surface area is 13.8 square miles. This depth to surface ratio keeps the lake's temperatures colder than other Finger Lakes. The thermocline will establish itself in the area of 35 to 40 feet below the surface at mid-August while the thermocline on Cayuga and Seneca lakes, for example, will more often be in the 90-foot range.

The colder water has other influences. Fish do not grow as rapidly as in warmer water. The richness of the fish-supporting aquatic life — both phytoplankton (micro-plants) and zoo-plankton (micro-animals) — is also less. Limiting plankton was an early objective of the City of Syracuse Water Authority, and if nature did not take care of it, the lake was treated with copper sulfate. The last chemical treatment was carried out in 1972.

Unlike most of the other Finger Lakes the forage base in Skaneateles Lake consists of neither smelt nor alewives. It is limited to yellow perch, golden shiners, sculpin and cisco (lake herring). The cisco, a plankton feeder reaching 8 to 12 inches in size, quickly grows to a size that prevents all but the largest fish from using it as forage.

Skaneateles is a cold lake, and there is little shallow water; most of the shoreline cascades to the lake at angles just shy of cliffs. Shallow, weed-filled habitat is limited to small areas at the northern and southern tips of the lake.

The main sport fish in Skaneateles are trout, salmon and smallmouth bass. Fishing for trout and salmon on Skaneateles Lake takes some adjustments. You need to forget about using the larger sized lures. Tiny silver spoons such as the Sutton 5 or the silver plated small Stinger (Tamiron #1), no more than two inches long, are the answer. You might on special days go as large as a 44 flutter spoon, but that is the largest. Most of the trout sustain themselves on cisco, perch or their own progeny.

The necessity of small baits seems to be associated with the

A small but high quality launch facility typical of those found on the Finger Lakes. This one, on Skaneateles Lake, has parking for about 30 vehicles and trailers.

lack of alewives (sawbellies) a bait that may not even legally be possessed on this lake. DEC did try to introduce smelt in 1927 and again in 1964 but both attempts failed.

Lake trout are now self-sustaining. Stocking of Seneca Lake strain lake trout was significant between 1942 and 1970, but was stopped because of a concern that the gamefish might become overpopulated in relation to the available forage. The lake trout became less numerous when the stocking was stopped, but they have since improved in size. In 1980 landlocked salmon were added to the cold water program to add diversity and trophy potential for anglers.

Rainbow trout successfully spawn in the lake's three significant tributaries: Grout Brook, Bear Swamp Creek and Shotwell Brook. They are also supplemented with annual stocking. Rainbow trout are an exciting fish, and winter anglers fishing from the city wall and dock in Skaneateles with marshmallows and corn are rewarded with fast runs and aerial antics that make these fish so popular. Landlocked salmon egg plantings have been made in Grout and Bear Swamp creeks in hopes of developing a natural reproduction cycle. Brown trout have not been stocked since 1993 because of poor returns.

There appears to be a very sensitive balance between stocking and the forage base. When the number of trout and salmon are too abundant the size of fish in the angler's creel drops significantly. While there are always a few trophies such as 15 pound lake trout and 10 pound rainbows and salmon, the average fish taken are much smaller and take longer to catch relative to many of the other Finger Lakes.

The average lake trout taken over the past ten years has remained at under two pounds. Rainbow trout and landlocked salmon have remained quite consistent at 1½ pounds each.

The average 2 hours of fishing effort it takes to catch one legal salmonid here may be the result of a number of factors. The prohibition against the use of alewives for bait requires that you change your tactics. The ban eliminates a major angling method: still fishing with live or frozen-and-thawed sawbellies, so productive in the other lakes.

Small lures, also critical to success on this water, may not be available to visiting anglers. They are not a common item in most tackle boxes. Anglers have, at best, limited supplies. And even local shops are not well stocked to support this requirement. You will want a sizeable supply of small spoons to be able to set out a "school" of lures as described in Chapter 4.

The steep-sided ledges in the lake are also difficult to fish. These areas attract an abundance of fish, but the highly irregular bottom makes it difficult to work your lures on or near the bottom without losing lots of tackle, including downrigger bombs or Seth Green rigs.

This type of bottom protects the normally vulnerable lake trout that hold tight to the bottom. Skaneateles Lake is the only Finger Lake where anglers take a higher percentage of rainbow trout than lake trout. I would suggest that the anglers are just raising their lures to conserve their tackle, thereby passing over the easier to catch lake trout. I would also suggest that the limited access blocks a great many of the serious anglers who might otherwise trailer to this pristine water. And, that many cottage owners included in the diary surveys are more casual anglers than those who specifically set out for a full-day of angling.

Aside from the DEC site, there is a free village boat access at Mandana on Route 41A. But the parking there is limited, and the launch is capable of handling only small boats. If you get into trouble, the adjacent marina is willing to help, but at a price.

Three other commercial access sites are at the south end of the lake. But these are limited to relatively small boats because of shallow water or steep approaches to the facility. DEC has 100 yards of undeveloped shoreline at the mouth of Grout Brook on the south end of the lake and this provides the only shore angling access other than the city pier and seawall in Skaneateles. There is no public access on the east side of the lake.

Fortunately, the 12 mile run to the southern waters from the DEC launch site mentioned earlier is relatively easy. The high banks and a prevailing west wind keep this water relatively protected. But you can also forego the run south and still have good trout fishing, beginning immediately south of the launch.

Fishing for trout in this lake provides the opportunity to take them on mayfly or scud (freshwater shrimp) imitations. These are an important food source for all of the salmonids, and in stomach survey work were found to represent as much as 16 to 38 percent of their total food by volume. Fly casting to surface feeding trout in the evening hours of late May and June can be a rare lake fishing treat.

Casting jigs over the rubble points can also produce a mixed creel of salmonids. White hair or white Mr. Twister plastic bodies are the rule for this kind of fishing. Normally you will be working in 20 to 30 feet of water.

Smallmouth bass are established in just about every shoreline area of the lake. They will hold against the rock ledges, and your success will often depend on just how close to shore you can stay with your baits and lures. It is also possible that you may bring in a mixed creel of bass, rainbow and brown trout and even an occasional landlocked salmon.

The salmonids will often cruise the same ledges looking for food. I met one young angler who was making a mad dash across the lake but who stopped just long enough to tell me he had been casting for bass several miles south of Mandana and had lost the biggest fish he had ever had in his life. A rainbow trout longer than his arm had taken his only sinking black and silver Rapala.

The average size smallmouth in Skaneateles is smaller than in other lakes. The lake's 10 inch size limit as compared to a 12 inch limit on the rest of the Finger Lakes reflects this growth limitation.

Perch are also small here compared to other lakes, with an average size seldom exceeding 10 inches. They will often be caught by anglers fishing for smallmouth, but you may want to concentrate on perch by working the northern and southern weed beds in the spring and fall of the year. Because of the clarity of the water you will have to anchor back from your fishing spot and depend on long casts. Either that or fish deeper than normal to keep from spooking your fish.

Skaneateles Lake should not be shunned as being second class. The pristine beauty that combines with acceptable angling makes this a unique and worthwhile fishing experience.

Chapter 6
CONESUS LAKE
by C. Scott Sampson

The fish rolled and flashed its tooth-filled mouth back and forth. I could see the spinner blade sticking out of the mouth just left of center, as if the fish had taken a dainty nip at the black-hair-skirted Mepps Giant Killer as it passed by the weed line that was only a shadow in the early morning light.

I was thinking I would hang up for sure casting so close to the weeds, but that is the most productive water. I let the lure sink out of sight. It stopped before it ever reached the 12 foot depth that I was looking for, and I pulled back.

The boil of water just inside the dark shadow confirmed I was into a good sized northern. He could shake and roll all he wanted to. As long as I could keep the lure centered and the line away from those teeth, I would win.

The fish was still thrashing in the net bag when I put the scale through the nylon loops. Just over 10 pounds, according to the bobbing needle. Needle-noised pliers retrieved my skirted hook, and I flipped the net upside down. The pike splashed me with the cool fall water in thanks for its freedom.

Conesus Lake is one of the best choices in the Finger Lakes for northern pike. Every year it gives up trophies in the 15 to 20-pound class. The 18.5 miles of shoreline on the 7.8 mile long lake offer tempting weed beds along nearly every inch. This is especially true in the fall of the year when anglers can troll or cast for these monsters in relative solitude.

From Memorial Day to Labor Day you can fish the very early hours. But after 9 a.m. the 4.97 square miles of surface water belong to local residents, thousands of them.

The lake and surroundings are highly populated. It is within 30 minutes of Rochester and connected by an arterial highway that delivers the city people almost to the edge of the lake. The surrounding shoreline is relatively flat, and was easily developed.

Conesus Lake has a long history of being the local playground. At the turn of the century, daily trains delivered vacationers to the railroad pier in Lakeville. As many as five steamboats cruised the lake at one time to take the excursionists on tours of the "always beautiful" Finger Lake.

With a maximum depth of 66 feet, the lake should offer an ideal combination of habitat for both cold and warm water species. But historically the lack of oxygen in the lower levels during the summer time has killed any opportunity for lake trout. And previous stockings of rainbow trout by the DEC have also proven a failure.

The tiger muskie, a sterile hybred, has been stocked since 1991 and is providing diversity to this cool water fishery.

For years Conesus was a fish factory for walleye, perch and bass. Ice fishing for perch was especially popular, and any sunlit winter day would bring thousands of anglers to the ice. The majority of them went home with more than enough perch for dinner.

DEC estimates those winter harvests were upwards of 175,000 fish, and anglers rated this lake second only to Oneida and Chautauqua Lakes for this "yellow gold." Considering the relative size of this lake, the perch fishing was nothing short of spectacular.

As the search for gold became a social problem in California and Alaska, the search for yellow perch became a major problem for winter residents on the lake shore. As the word spread, anglers converged on the lake. Parking was limited, and many simply abandoned their cars along the side of the

road and headed for the ice. The Livingston County Sheriff's Department finally had to tow anglers' cars away to clear the roads.

Everyone caught fish in those early years and lots of them. The late Marco DeSio and his sons Don and Ed made the trip from their home in Waterloo to Conesus nearly every Wednesday and Sunday of the winter months. They counted their catches of perch by the hundreds.

The glory road of perch fishing came to an abrupt end. The fishery crashed. Generally the demise of the lake is blamed on the introduction of the alewife or sawbelly either in 1979 or 1980, by persons unknown. The competition for zooplankton with the perch, combined with the fact that sawbellies will eat perch and walleye fry, was the official explanation from DEC for the dramatic decline of both perch and walleye populations. Walleye are now responding to the stocking of hatchery fingerlings.

Is Conesus Lake dead? Not by a long shot. It certainly had its problems, witness the fact that the one and only bait shop was about to close. But the fisheries crash may have actually been a blessing. It provided a breather to the social problems of too many anglers, especially in the winter months. There was a nearly 30-fold decrease in the ice fishing pressure from the Golden Days, according to Bill Abraham, chief of fisheries for Region 8. The crash provided time for the development of additional public access to the lake to prevent future conflicts. Today, Conesus has the best public access per acre of water of any of the Finger Lakes.

A state launch site off East Lake Road, just south of McPherson Point, offers parking for 70 vehicles and trailers and also has well maintained public rest rooms. A small boat ramp and car top fishing access site at the southwest corner of the lake, off Route 256, can handle another 40 vehicles. A large parking lot just west of the Conesus Outlet on Pebble Beach Road, principally developed for ice anglers, is also open for car top boats launched in the Outlet. A public park at Sand Point, locally called Vitale Park, on the north end is jointly operated by DEC and the Town of Livonia. It offers ice fishing access in the winter and swimming and shore angling in the summer. There is a car top launch with parking for 45 cars.

The massive population explosion of the alewife that probably caused the fishery crash now seems to be leveling. The large alewives are gone and the remainder are small and show signs of stress. Small die-offs have also occurred as the various biological communities within the lake adjust to the interactions of nature. Perch have returned in good numbers, though perhaps not the equal of pre-crash days. They are also small, even at age four, indicating the strong competition for food. Walleye populations are regaining their former numbers, but are more difficult to catch because of the abundance of forage fish.

Bass, both largemouth and smallmouth, and northern pike offer the best quality warm water fishing, says Abraham. An angler can reasonably expect to catch four pound largemouth

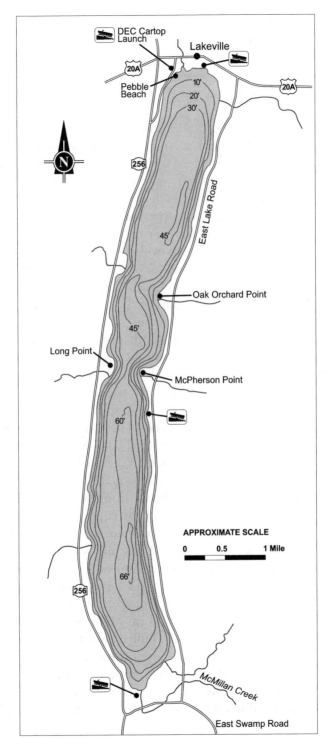

Figure 6.1 Conesus Lake

bass, three pound smallmouth and 10 pound northern pike from this water.

The turnaround continues, and some are betting the final result will be a more balanced fishery than before the crash. The alewife in the forage base seems to have added pounds on resident fish. Twelve pound walleye and 20 pound pike are trophies from any water, and each year some lucky anglers have these dream-making angling experiences.

The alewife has changed some fishing habits. In the fall of the year northern pike anglers will now troll the edge of the weedbeds with silver spoons on shallow set downriggers, rather than with the more traditional Creek Chub Pikie minnow.

Walleye fishing in the spring of the year, before the crash, was limited to the traditional method of drifting bait with rigs such as bait walkers in the deeper southern waters of the lake. The fish would wait there to gobble up the natural foods riding the currents of Conesus Inlet, a 30 mile stretch of stream that passes through significant wetlands. Today many successful anglers are using Lake Erie methods for catching suspended walleye.

Deep running, large-billed crank baits such as the Bomber A series, Cordell Wally Diver, Hot 'N Tot and Thunderstick are being run 150 to 200 feet behind the boat. Running these lures off a planer is even better as walleye tend to shy away from boats. These lures are different from the natural alewife, which may be of assistance in calling attention to the lure. Suspended walleye fishing should be concentrated in the deep central portion of the lake, between Long and McPherson points and further south. The large billed crankbaits on 10 pound test line will dive to 25 feet, too deep to attempt fishing along the shoreline structure without hanging up all the time.

Planer boards are set out on heavy line or cord at a fixed distance from the boat. They are pulled away from the boat by the design of the plane as it moves through the water. The connecting cord, held tight over the water, now provides a platform to hold the line releases much in the same manner as a downrigger cable except out to the side of the boat. The releases are free to slide down the planer cord until stopped by the angler controlling the fishing line at the reel. The releases are most often friction devices that hold the fishing line as set by the angler until the strength of the strike pulls it free of the release and the side-planer.

You can set out up to three lines to a side-planer, but keep all the lures the same on each side of the boat for fewer tangles. Even then, you want to maintain maximum spacing. You should also plan your turns to be wide and easy so you don't spend the rest of your fishing time respooling your reels.

In the early spring look for schools of bait in warm pocket water, in the range of 62 degrees. In the summer months you might try using downriggers to reach the suspended walleye that will lay just above the thermocline. Spoons, including some salmon favorites like the Northern King 28, will take these fish.

Some of the best fishing in the lake is within rowing distance of the boat launch site. Perch and other panfish are concentrated in the spring and fall off Long Point, as well as the structure between McPherson and Old Orchard Points. Brown jigs or fathead minnows on small gold hooks will take the fish. They should be fished just outside the weed line in 15 to 18 feet of water.

Northern pike and walleye spawn in the marsh areas of the Conesus Inlet Wildlife Management Area on the south end of the lake. When the season opens in early May, they will still be in the waters south of the boat launch. Casting the traditional spoons, spinners or stickbaits to the weedlines or just over the weeds should bring the desired results. Large spinner baits normally used for bass will also attract northern pike.

Largemouth bass seem to control the northern waters of the lake. Fishing the weedbeds with traditional baits such as the plastic worm, spinnerbaits, plastic grubs and jigs can account for limits on any given morning. Remember to start at sunrise to avoid the crowds.

Smallmouth bass are found concentrated more at mid-lake off the structures of Old Orchard, Long and McPherson Points.

Use crankbaits in the early season, and jigs or live bait fished progressively deeper as the water warms.

In the fall, besides casting for northern pike, you might want to drift with live bait under bobbers. Use large chubs or golden shiners along the edge of the weeds. Some of the largest trophies will be taken this way.

Ice fishing will normally begin about Christmas week on this relatively shallow lake. Most fishing will start in the northern waters or in the central region of the lake. Be very cautious about the ice thickness in the southern end of the lake. The warm waters from the inlet can make this dangerous at almost any time of the winter.

Northern pike, walleye and bass can all be taken with the use of fathead minnows or golden shiners for bait. Perch are more often taken on jigs tipped with mousie or oak leaf grubs. Stopping at Bob's Bait and Tackle in Lakeville on Routes 15 and 20A, the only angler service on the lake, will give you the latest information. If you are in doubt, just follow the crowds. Ice anglers are a friendly lot. Just don't cut your hole on top of theirs.

Ice fishing can be productive in depths from five to 40 feet. Often an angler will cut his holes in a line working progressively deeper with each hole. You are currently allowed five tip-ups and two hand lines, but be sure to check the newest "New York State Fishing Regulations Guide" before going fishing. If one depth becomes productive then cluster your tip-ups at the same depth.

Portable depth finders may be helpful. If you take one along, you might consider using a motorcycle battery as a power source. The battery is compact yet powerful, and totally sealed for leak-proof operation. It can also be recharged with the normal auto-battery charger you use on marine or car batteries.

Cold weather can tax an energy source, so it is best to start the day with a full charge. GBN, manufacturer of marine and recreational batteries, suggests that a simple but accurate voltmeter will tell the condition of a battery's charge before going on the ice, or open water for that matter. A fully charged battery should measure 12.6 volts; 75 percent charge is 12.4; 50 percent, 12.2; 25 percent, 12.0 and a discharged battery will register just below 12 at 11.9 volts. Because of narrow measurement tolerance, be sure to zero your meter before taking these measurements.

Chapter 7
OWASCO LAKE
by C. Scott Sampson

"T he great thing about Owasco Lake is the fishing is good in all areas," said Captain Bill Haessner who calls both Cayuga and Owasco Lakes his home waters. "Larger lakes, like Cayuga, have hot spots such as in the spring of the year when landlocked salmon and brown trout are concentrated in the south end of the lake," continued Haessner who specializes in light tackle for salmonids. "But not Owasco. If you don't find them (trout and salmon) on one side of the lake they are on the other."

This 11.1 mile long lake is ideal cold water habitat with a mean depth of 97 feet and a maximum depth of 180 feet. It is a typical glacial lake with shallow waters at the north and south ends. The east and west shores have steep sided ledges that are ideal smallmouth habitat, and ideal structure for holding trout and salmon.

There are some exceptions to the fast drop-offs. One is between Seward and Adams Points on the southeast shore. Another is just south of Burtis Point. Both areas are good prospects for northern pike fishing, as are the southern shallows.

Owasco Lake is fed principally by the Owasco Inlet and tributaries to that water. The tributaries of Dutch Hollow Creek, Sucker Brook and Long Point Creek are minor in comparison, but at certain times of the year become important to the angler. All the streams are considered too warm for successful trout reproduction, and competition with smallmouth bass limits even the marginal reproductive success cold water species experience here. That is not to say the salmonids do not try. The tributaries are important for angling in the spring and fall of the year as rainbows, browns, and salmon attempt to spawn, despite the poor habitat.

The cold water fishery depends on the annual stocking that averages 40,000 fingerlings or the equivalent per year. The stocking once included the seeforellen brown trout, a European strain that has been said to have the potential of growing to over 50 pounds. The strain had been stocked for several years in Owasco since 1985, but no major difference was detected between that strain and the domestic browns that have been a part of the lake fishery since the early '70s. Only domestic browns are now stocked.

Lake trout, the most popular species in the lake, were stocked as early as 1884. Rainbow trout were stocked in 1910 and steelhead ten years later. In the early days Owasco also supported walleye and cisco. But like so many of the Finger Lakes, those fisheries collapsed with the establishment of smelt. In Owasco, smelt were first stocked in 1925. The last good walleye fishing dates back to pre-1950. But the Owasco Lake Anglers Association has stocked walleye since 1996 with at least limited success. The walleye are pond raised to a size of 3 to 4 inches in length before stocking, thus avoiding the conflict with smelt and alewives.

Northern pike and the alewife appeared in Owasco in the early 60s, no doubt from individuals doing their own stocking. The black crappie is also thought to have been introduced in this manner, and is now showing up in the shallow waters of the southern end of the lake.

Owasco Lake has better than average fishing opportunity and its proximity to population centers should make it popular. However, public access is limited and the Auburn City Council had further restricted the access to Owasco in the name of protecting its city water supply from zebra mussels. A law passed in the spring of 1991, but since recinded, required a boat be steam cleaned prior to launching.

Just south of the City of Auburn off Route 38A is Emerson Park, a county facility that is located on the Owasco Outlet as well as the northern shore of the lake. Boat size is limited on this launch because you must pass under a foot bridge that will block access for boats in the 22 foot class with any kind of cabin or canvas structure.

On the south end of the lake off Route 38 is Grany's Lakeside Country Outdoors, formerly the South Shore Marina. This is the only facility currently on the south end of the lake. It has a double launch with docks on either side, a configuration that's especially helpful in dealing with the wind. Boats of up to 25 feet will find this facility an ideal means for access to the southern waters such as Ensenore Point, one of the areas off which both lake trout and browns seem to congregate. Fall stocking of brown trout takes place here. It is also one of the more productive areas on the lake for ice fishing.

To the east of the outlet at Martin Point is a town house development. It can be used as a guide to quality smallmouth fishing, including some up to six pounds. Actually, the entire north end of the lake is excellent bass fishing, as are the waters on the east side south of Martin all the way to Long Point. White plastic jigs are the top producing bass bait on this water.

The cold water fishery has become more consistent over the years, and there has been a steady decrease in the hours of effort necessary to catch a legal salmonid. It is now in the range of 2 hours while just 10 years ago the average was closer to three hours. In those early days, Owasco seemed to be a boom or bust water. In the early spring, still fishing using live sawbellies accounted for limits of lake trout. The hotspot was in the north end of the lake off Buck and Peterson Points in 40 to 50 feet of water. Today there is more hardware angling and trolling for suspended fish.

Still fishing will usually assure you a limit of 1½ to three pound lake trout. The technique is both effective and inexpensive from the standpoint of tackle. Basic equipment is an open faced spinning system, a barrel sinker about one ounce in size, snap swivel, rubber band, a few English style bait hooks, a bait needle and a half-dozen smelt or sawbellies. The English style bait hook or a long snelled double hook is threaded with the bait needle just under the skin and along the dorsal fin of the bait so the hooks are pointing toward the tail of the bait. The hook points should be just over the head or behind the eye of the bait.

The free moving barrel sinker is put on your line, followed by the snap swivel. Sometimes anglers will place a glass bead on the line above the snap swivel to protect the knot from sticking in the sinker, but this is not a necessity. The snap swivel is just a quick method of attaching the snelled bait hook, as well as acting as the sinker stop.

The free-moving weight allows the trout to pick up the bait and move off with it without feeling resistance. That is the critical thing for this style of fishing. Lake trout will not swallow the bait immediately but will take it sideways in their mouth and move off, away from other fish. Only then is the bait turned head first in the trout's mouth and swallowed. Any resistance, and the trout will drop the bait.

In addition to the slip sinker you will want to fish with an open bail on your spinning rod. The rubber band goes around your rod in front of the reel to gently hold a loop of line so that you can tell when a trout has picked up your offering. Some anglers will also use a small piece of tin foil pinched on the line at the tip of the rod as a strike flag to signal a pickup. Only when the line starts to move the second time do you close the bail and set the hook.

An alternative to the heavy slip sinker still fishing method is to add two to four small split shot on your line three feet above the bait. The idea is to put just enough weight on so the minnow swims slowly to the bottom passing through the zones of water that may hold browns, rainbows or salmon before it reaches the depth for lake trout. The amount of split shot should

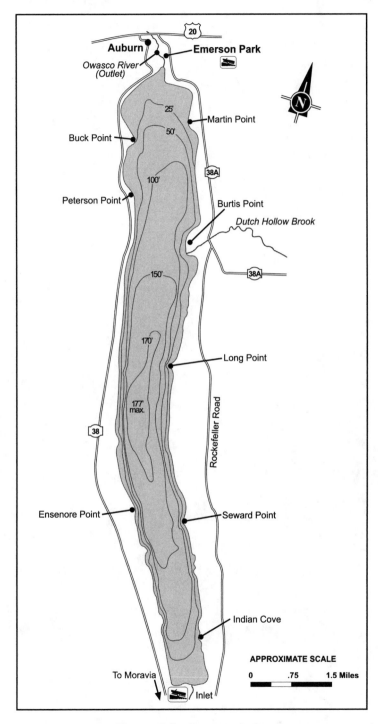

Figure 7.1 Owasco Lake

be very slight, almost reaching neutral buoyancy with the bait so lake trout will not feel the weight. Steve Walker of Rushville was one of the first to use this technique in the Finger Lakes. Those who have tried it term it as "deadly," and they consistently take a mixed creel of salmonids.

If there is a problem with still fishing, it is the fact that it is more difficult to release a fish if it is under the 15-inch minimum length. You will have to cut the hook snell as close to the mouth as possible and leave the hook in the fish. The stomach acids will make quick work of the hook within a week with apparently few adverse side effects.

Consistently larger fish, from five to eight-pound lake trout, may more frequently be caught by trolling. Once the thermocline sets up in the summer the largest trout seem to concentrate below the sharp temperature drop that separates the warm surface waters from the cold bottom layers. Downrigger anglers have taken them from depths of 130 to 140 feet. Above the thermocline it is not unusual to take four and five pound rainbows, landlocked salmon and brown trout.

Small spoons generally work better than large ones. Haessner's most productive lure has been an F3 Evil Eye, a three-inch flutter spoon in two-tone green and with a silver lightening bolt. My own successes come mostly from fishing the ledges on the east and west shores. Using standard size Stinger spoons I take mixed creels of rainbow, landlocked salmon and brown trout.

This relatively small lake can produce some big fish. This past season a lake trout of 15 pounds was taken from Owasco, and historical records show several 20 pound lake trout have been boated. Day in and day out Owasco will produce a lake trout of about 4 pounds. The average rainbow trout taken is 3 pounds, browns four pounds and landlocked salmon three pounds.

Chapter 8
HEMLOCK &
CANADICE LAKES
by C. Scott Sampson

Within the rolling hills of the Finger Lakes region, dotted with farms, small towns and cities, there are the small wilderness-like areas encompassing Hemlock and Canadice Lakes.

Both lakes are relatively small, and both are surrounded by forests that are a part of a controlled watershed environment. There are no shoreline cottages to mar the wilderness view. Water recreation is limited to fishing only and that too is controlled by annual permit. Even the size of the boats and motors are controlled. Boats must be no more than 16 feet in length and motors not more than 10 h.p.

The watershed permit is free, but it is necessary. You may pick up an annual permit at a self-service registration desk at the Hemlock administration area just south of the Town of Hemlock. Follow the signs at Rix Hill Road off Route 15A. The permit is good for both lakes.

The lakes are well patrolled and anyone without the permit will be prosecuted. The permit is a very minor inconvenience to the angler, but it maintains control over the number of persons using the areas, an important consideration since these waters are so close to populations counted in the millions. The larger of the two lakes, Hemlock, receives an estimated 30,000 annual fishing trips while the smaller Canadice Lake has nearly

35,000 annual angler trips.

Canadice Lake is only about three miles long as compared to Hemlock Lake at seven miles in length, but it has better fishing access than Hemlock. Canadice Lake Road, off Route 20A, runs the entire length of the east side of the lake and is within walking distance of the lake. Anglers can shore fish almost the entire east side or use the launch site that is located about mid-lake off the same road near the intersection with Birch Hill Road.

HEMLOCK LAKE

Hemlock Lake has two launch sites: one at the north end of the lake and one at the south end. While Route 15A runs the full length of this lake, it does not come close to the lake shore nor is it convenient to hike the massive hill to the lake proper. As a result, the shore fishing is much more limited here.

The northern launch site on Hemlock is easy to find. Just south of the Town of Hemlock on Route 15A you come to Rix Hill Road. Follow the signs to the launch that is just over a mile from the Rix Hill intersection and down a dirt road that follows the eastern shore of the lake. The southern launch is also off 15A, just past the Livingston County line. A pull-off turns into a dirt and gravel road that doubles back along the lake shore. In late summer and fall, however, this launch may not be usable as the lake level drops. The shallowness of the lake at this location can leave you on a shelf of mud with no way to the lake.

Hemlock Lake has an annual fluctuation of 5.8 feet, but the water authority has the capability to draw the lake down 15.3 feet below its maximum surface height. The annual level variance for Canadice is 4.3 feet with the lowest levels occurring between November 15 and January 1.

Hemlock Lake, at seven miles in length and a half-mile across, is relatively small by Finger Lakes standards. It has a mean depth of 45 feet and a maximum depth of 91 feet. The lake is steep sided, and has less than 10 percent of its water in

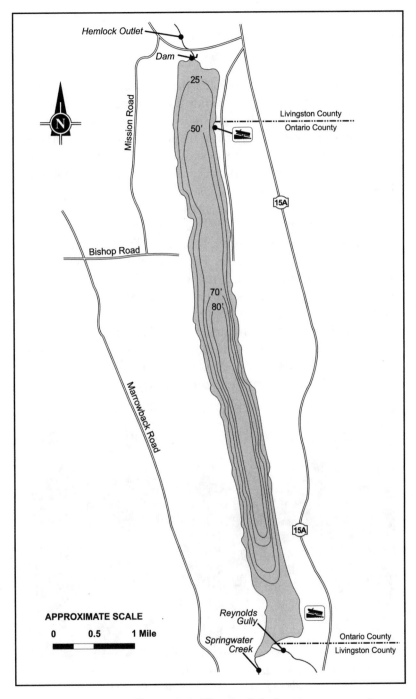

Figure 8.1 Hemlock Lake

the littoral zone (water that is less than 20 feet deep). The lake stratifies, or develops a thermocline during the summer months and provides superior habitat for cold water species such as lake trout, rainbow trout, brown trout and landlocked salmon. Brook trout are no longer stocked in Hemlock, but you may find a trophy fish or two from a small native brook trout population found in the Reynold's Gulf Brook, a tributary. This stream, which enters the lake at the southeast corner, is only 2.5 miles long and averages just 12 feet across.

Smallmouth bass, pickerel, perch, and limited largemouth bass are also found in the lake. The pickerel growth rate in this water is, according to DEC records, one of the best in the state. Perhaps it is the abundance of the forage base that includes smelt, alewives and golden shiners.

A similar rapid growth rate occurs in Hemlock's lake trout. The average size lake trout taken far surpasses any other Finger Lake or even Lake Ontario. A six year old lake trout can weigh as much as 10 pounds while in other waters a laker of that size

Hemlock Lake, a reservoir for Rochester, can fluctuate in level a significant number of feet during the year. A free permit is necessary to fish this scenic Finger Lake.

would be eight to even ten years of age. While the number of lake trout caught is not high, the average one from Hemlock Lake has been consistently above five pounds for the last ten years, and has averaged as high as 8.1 pounds. An angler can reasonably expect to take lake trout of 10 plus pounds, and some as large as 16 pounds are taken from this lake each year. The average number of hours needed to catch a legal trout or salmon has also remained relatively low over the last ten years, averaging just over four hours (in recent years, as low as 2.5 hours). An average of three to four hours of fishing effort to catch a legal salmonid is considered an acceptable level of success by fishery managers, based on angler satisfaction surveys.

With the exception of the rainbow trout which depends on natural reproduction from Spring Creek, the Hemlock Lake fishery is supported by stocking. Annually, just under 20,000 cold water fish are stocked here.

The brown trout, first stocked in 1983, has become one of the more popular targets of angling opportunity, and now is the salmonid most frequently found in the angler's creel. Browns will average just under three pounds in size, but one of eight plus pounds is possible. Landlocked salmon are also a relatively new introduction, having been first stocked in 1975. They are the second most popular species and make up a major portion of the salmonids kept by anglers.

Because anglers tend to concentrate on both brown trout and landlocked salmon here, flat line trolling is an important fishing method. This is especially true in the spring and fall, when these two species seek the warmest available water. Even in the summer months they will remain above the thermocline, in waters that range from 56 to 62 degrees. Long leaders and light lines will also increase your catch rate. One very successful brown trout angler uses an electric trolling motor because of its minimal noise. Planer boards are also recommended for this relatively shallow kind of fishing.

Stickbaits such as the Rapala in black and silver or orange and gold are successful lures, but don't overlook the use of spoons such as the silver Suttons or even the Little Cleo. In the summer months the use of multi-leader thermocline equipment or Seth Green rigs allow an angler to cover a wider column of water, and is a very successful method for cold water angling when the trout are suspended in a variety of water temperatures.

Warm water fishing, especially smallmouth bass fishing with lures and live bait along the shore structure, can often result in a mixed creel of bass, trout, perch and other panfish. Fishing with worms is also a major means of catching trout on this water. Normally it is done in 25 to 30 feet of water in the summer months. Don't overlook the soft shelled crayfish or crab as a bait for summer smallmouth.

Historical records for Hemlock show that the lake once supported an abundance of walleye. That species is non-existent now, as is true in the other Finger Lakes where smelt and alewives were introduced into the forage base.

CANADICE LAKE

Canadice Lake is more wilderness-like than Hemlock. Even getting there is an adventure over country roads that sometimes look more like back-woods trails. Perhaps it's this factor, combined with better shore access, that accounts for Canadice's popularity.

Interestingly, Canadice is the more difficult lake to fish when judged by the number of hours needed to catch a legal salmonid. Over the past five years that has been well above 4.0, generally considered the acceptable level for angler satisfaction. But, I have never heard a complaint. Anglers I speak with hold this lake in special reverence. It has its own special beauty and peace, an appeal borne of the wilderness atmosphere. Even the Department of Health's warning not to eat any lake or brown trout over 21 inches because of a toxic PCB chemical spill does not deter anglers. The spill, by the way, came from an individual taking electric transformers apart for salvage.

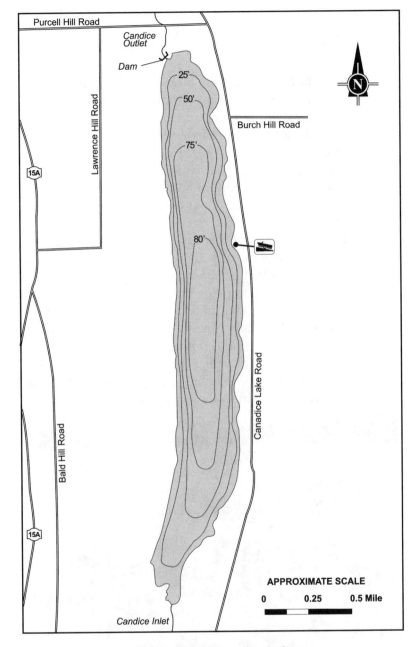

Figure 8.2   Canadice Lake

Anglers will often target the more abundant smallmouth bass, and fish for trout and salmon only when the time is just right. This may be in the spring or fall when the fish are near the surface and susceptible to surface trolling or casting.

Canadice is the smallest of all the Finger Lakes, being only three miles long and a half-mile wide. It has a mean depth of 54 feet and a maximum depth of 83 feet. There are no major tributaries and its watershed drains only 12 square miles.

In spite of the poor catch rate for trout the opportunity still exists, and the average size lake trout from Canadice is larger than on many of the other Finger Lakes. The lake trout you catch will more often be above five pounds than below it. Lakers of 10 pounds are not especially unusual.

The small size of the lake adds to the intimate feeling you get here. Its relatively shallow depth makes it ideal for pulling copper line, a technique that is both personal and productive. You hand-line your lure, bumping the bottom of the lake with a variety of terminal lures including a Pflueger Record spoon (no longer made) or Barracuda single hooked spoon, Twin

Boat size is limited on Canadice Lake. Access is via an unimproved shore launch.

Minnow, FlatFish or even a flasher or lake troll unit with bait or a spoon at the end.

The copper line, normally a single strand of 30 pound test, will often be reeled on an "H" hand reel or, if you were lucky enough to have an old-time record player, on an auto-windup reel made with the old Victrola record player spring motor. Special Victrola boxes are constructed with a 16 mm movie reel for a spool to hold the copper line. As you pull the line and hopefully a fish toward the boat, the line is automatically reeled onto the film spool. There are also electric reels of similar fashion, but they never met with the popularity of the Victrola boxes that are still in use today.

Without an auto reel of some sort, the angler with the hand "H" or similar line holding device does not reel in his line. He simply loops the copper line at his feet as he brings his fish in. The secret is not to move your feet or the copper line until it can be let back into the water. The angler's fear is tangling or forming a kink in his line. Any sharp bend in the copper, if not repaired by cutting it and inserting a brass swivel, will result in a line break sooner or later. That means the loss of your tackle or, worse yet, a trophy-sized trout and your tackle.

The modern copper angler normally wears a leather finger guard to protect the index finger where the copper line runs. The old-time anglers often had a thick callus on that edge of their finger, and a groove in the callus where the line would ride as they "jerked" it off the bottom with each motion or pull of their arm. The success of this method relies on the lure stirring the bottom mud, forming little clouds as bait fish might do as they feed along the bottom. Lake trout simply cannot resist this invitation and when using Twin Minnows and FlatFish, I have had lake trout fully engulf the lure in their eagerness to feed.

Some anglers will use a short monofilament leader of three feet at the end of the copper line, in part to be less visible than the copper but also to act as an insurance policy against the loss of the more expensive copper line should the lure hang up.

Catching fish with a handheld copper line is an exciting method of fishing. You feel every boulder on the bottom of the lake as you troll the line. And when you have a fish on, its raw power is telegraphed to your hands with a feeling that is often blocked, even by the most sensitive rods. You are in control. You give and take line during the battle, your arm acting as the shock absorber. And it is your ability to recognize the fish's power and give it line at the proper time that prevents the hook from being pulled free. You will lose a good many fish before you are proficient with this method but you will also have many more strikes than with other angling methods.

With copper line angling you do not need a depth finder. On Canadice that may be an advantage, given the boating restrictions. Your fingers and mind will chart the bottom.

Copper line angling can also be an ideal small boat angling method. An angler rowing the water can place the copper in a rowing hand and provide motion to the lure at the same time he is propelling the boat. He can also hold the copper in his paddle hand if he is fishing from a canoe.

Canadice Lake, because of its small size and also because it's at the highest elevation of any of the Finger Lakes, freezes first. It provides ice fishing opportunity for trout as well as the more traditional winter gamesters like pickerel, perch, bass and rock bass. Fathead minnows or golden shiners are recommended for most species except perch. They seem to prefer oak leaf or mousie grubs fished off small jigs and given action off a hand line or short jigging rod. The shallow ends of the lake seem more productive in the winter months than the steeper sided east and west shores.

Chapter 9
HONEOYE & OTISCO LAKES
by C. Scott Sampson

T he angler was thin enough to need split shot in his pockets during a stiff wind so I knew the 100 quart cooler in his boat was not just for holding his lunch. He was obviously one serious angler.

He was anchored off California Point on Honeoye Lake in 24 feet of water and using an ultra light graphite rod with a double perch rig. More often than not, he had both hooks loaded with crappie as he eased them over the side and into the cooler. He did it quietly, trying not to attract the attention of any of the more than 20 other boats working that immediate water. My graph finder was recording nearly a solid black line just a foot off the bottom. If you looked closely, you could see the individual marks of the inverted "V" that indicated fish.

He knew I had been watching him for some time, and when I asked how he was doing he admitted to OK. When I asked him what he was using he hesitated a little, but then shared his secret with me, perhaps hoping I would shut up and go away.

"White Mr. Twister jigs tipped with spikes," he said in a soft voice. Sound travels over water, and he seemed to be having the best action of any of the boats in the area.

The black crappie, by any of its ten or more names, still makes some fine eating. If you can keep them on a bed of ice, so much the better. On Honeoye Lake the locals use the term calico bass. On Cayuga Lake I hear strawberry bass being used and papermouth is a close second or third on almost any of the Finger Lakes waters.

Honeoye Lake is the second smallest of the Finger Lakes. Lying almost due south of Rochester it has become circled with homes and at times can be a high density recreational water. Interestingly enough, fishing seems to take a back seat to boating and swimming. Unlike most of the glacial lakes, Honeoye is shallow. It has a maximum depth of only 30 feet, and that is only in a relatively small portion of the lake located along the east side, south of Log Cabin or Burns Point and opposite California Point. The lake is really more like a bath tub 4.1 miles in length and ½ mile in width on average.

Its principal gamefish is the walleye. A good number of these fish are taken, but the degree of expertise necessary to be successful has many anglers shifting their attention to other,

Fisheries management policies are carefully tailored to the needs and holding capabilities of each individual Finger Lake. Many species in some of the lakes reproduce naturally, however. (Courtesy DEC)

more cooperative fish. Bass, perch and crappie seem to fill that niche. Not that any of these fish are necessarily easy to catch, but they seem easier than the more elusive walleye.

Night trolling for walleye is one of the major angling methods on Honeoye Lake. When the season first opens in May, productive trolling will be along the shoreline in only three to five feet of water. Stickbaits such as the Rapala and Rebel are used. And hang on to your rod because "pike" of 6 to 8 pounds are possible even though most will be smaller. The southern half of the lake is more productive than the northern half, and especially along the shore that parallels the deepest part of the lake. The average walleye for this water is in the 1½ to 3 pound category, and there is normally a good number of these fish.

As the season progresses, the walleye move to deeper waters. Night trolling with bait walkers or drag sinkers and live bait such as worms or leeches is still productive but the fish can now be taken during the day with slow trolled artificial stickbaits off downriggers. The lake is almost too small for anglers to use the side planer and crankbait techniques pioneered on Lake Erie for suspended fish. But don't rule it out, especially on a rain filled day when there is little to no boat traffic.

Sandy Schulman, a professional bass angler and Ranger Boat representative, calls Honeoye "a biological dream." Schulman is looking at it from the standpoint of a bass angler, and at the abundance of weed growth that surrounds the edges of the lake. Weeds are found wherever the water is less than 12 feet deep. In summer and fall, the area just north of Log Cabin Point is nearly a solid farm of weeds that can hold and protect largemouth bass of up to seven pounds. It takes a competent angler to entice one of those trophies out of its lair, but it is possible. At first light, use surface plugs, buzzbaits or even a spinnerbait whipped across the openings to bring out the more active fish. As the day brightens you will need to change to plastic worms that can be eased into an opening and allowed to flutter to the bottom.

There are also some smallmouth bass available, but in far

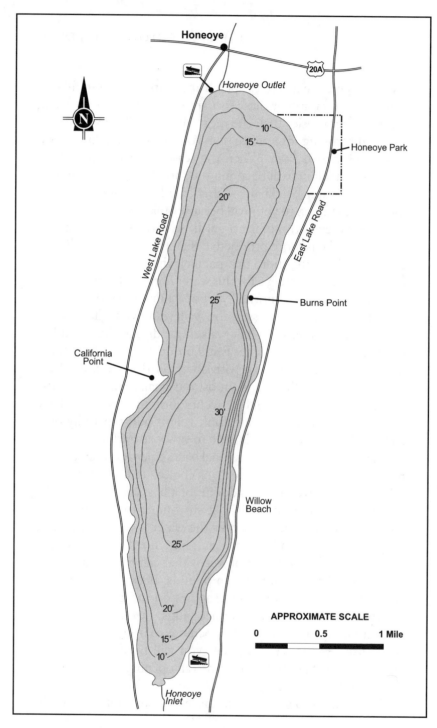

Figure 9.1   Honeoye Lake

fewer numbers than the largemouth. Smallmouth want bottom structure, a physical characteristic that this lake is short on with the possible exception of the area off California Point. That water is the best smallmouth location on the lake, and it also attracts nearly all other species at one time or another during the year. It is, in addition, a popular ice fishing locale for perch, crappie and an occasional walleye.

Access to the lake is via a double ramp launch site located in the southeastern portion of the lake off East Lake Road. The parking is limited to 35 vehicles and trailers. A private, gravel ramp is available for a fee at California Point and the facility called California Ranch. A municipal cartop launch is located on Sandy Bottom Road in the Village of Honeoye. Winter access to the lake is in short supply because of the extensive building along the shore. Most anglers will use the launch site parking and then walk or sled to their fishing grounds.

OTISCO LAKE

Otisco Lake may not appear to have a great deal in common with Honeoye Lake, but the fishing quality and methods are very similar. Otisco is also a small lake, just 5.4 miles in length and averaging just over a ½ mile wide. It has a maximum depth of 76 feet and an average depth of only 34 feet. Otisco stratifies in the summer months, but the lack of oxygen in the lower levels of the lake do not allow for the successful stocking of cold water species. The DEC has officially changed its management policy for this lake to a warm water fishery only. The Onondaga County Hatchery continues to stock Otisco Lake with approximately four to six thousand brown trout per year, but the DEC is limiting its stocking to walleye and the hybrid tiger musky.

* Note: In this book, cool water rather than warm water is used to denote such species as pike, black bass, pickerel, walleye, etc.

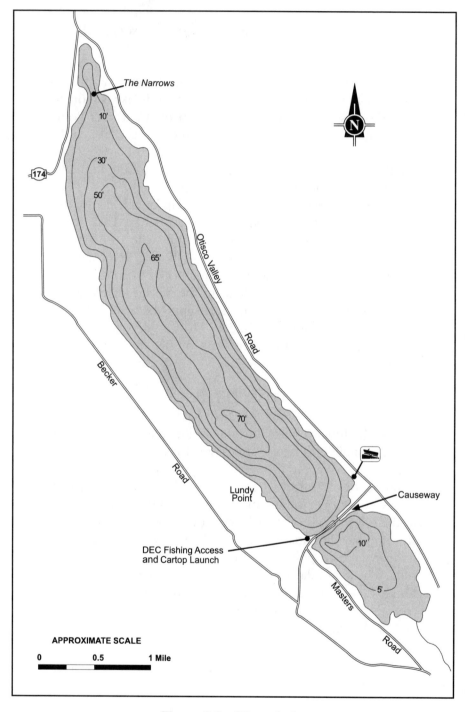

Figure 9.2   Otisco Lake

A causeway across Otisco Lake separates the lake into a comparatively shallow basin and a much deeper one. In the former (background), black bass hold forth. In the deeper basin, foreground, trout, walleye, smallmouth bass and tiger muskies can be caught.

Otisco is really two lakes because it is divided by a causeway that cuts across the southern portion of the lake. The southern impoundment, or pond as it is sometimes called, is a shallow silt-filled area of about 300 acres that has a mean depth of six feet and a maximum of 15 feet. It is important to the overall clarity of the main lake, however, because it acts as a settling bowl. While most fish at one time of year or another will find their way into the pond, the only important fishery here is for largemouth bass in the early season.

The channel through the causeway and the main lake side of the rip-rap that makes the separation are both important fishing areas. Anglers will find a DEC access site and cartop launch site on the west side of the causeway off Masters Road or West Valley Road, depending on the map you are looking at. Fishing with live bait, especially minnows, gives you the potential of catching nearly anything that swims in the lake including some lunker sized tiger muskies or a walleye of up to 12 pounds. A good deal of night fishing takes place at this location.

Otisco has a serious public access problem. The only boat launch available is a private ramp at Otisco Marine off Otisco Valley Road at the southeast corner of the main lake. Parking is limited, and fees reflect the lack of competition.

Fishing Otisco for walleye is difficult because the adult walleye population is limited and they have an abundance of feed. Recruitment of young walleye has been troubled because of competition between walleye fry and the illegally introduced alewife, which occurred in the mid-60s. There is also a major population of white perch, another combination baitfish-forage fish, and one that feeds on both zooplankton and young walleye.

A heavy stocking of brown trout was tried by DEC from 1969 to 1972 as a control measure for the alewife. And while some trophy browns were developed, the control did not work. The trout stocking continued, but in fewer numbers, until 1987. Tiger musky became the control fish of choice in 1977, and continues to be stocked. These, too, have reached trophy size of up to 20 pounds and Otisco is considered as some of the best tiger mucky fishing in the state.

The walleye continue to suffer from the competition of the alewife and white perch at the fry stage, when they are each feeding on the zooplankton forage base. DEC has found on other lakes with similar biological problems that fry stocking, even in massive numbers, is not the answer. Stocking at the yearling size is a better means of taking the walleye past that critical stage. The population continues to build.

Walleye fishing in Otisco, as in Honeoye Lake, is most productive at night. Trolling between the hours of 10 p.m. and 3 a.m. seems to be the most productive. Stickbaits or bait harnesses with worms are the most popular baits. Most anglers will work the southeast shoreline of the lake just north of the marina along the rip-rap wall. In the summer season the walleye suspend over deeper water in this same area and along the west side of the lake between Lundy and Lader Points.

Largemouth bass are caught using traditional methods. Anglers should work any weed areas, and especially those found along the causeway and the shorelines adjacent to it.

Smallmouth bass are a different story in this water. In the early season they will be on the shoreline and point structure. As summer progresses they move off the structure, and you will more often find them suspended and working the schools of bait. They will be in the upper 30 feet of water because oxygen levels below the thermocline are not conducive to any of the resident fish species. Small silver spoons, such as the Sutton 5 or Stinger number 1 by Tamiron, have produced smallmouth for Deiter Kraemer and myself from depths of 25 to 30 feet.

Fishing in this range with lures that imitate alewives can potentially bring you mixed creels of bass, trout and walleye. There may even be an occasional tiger musky, although most of these will be holding at the outer edge of the weed lines. They are also more inclined to take a minnow or a slowly worked jig.

Ice fishing on Otisco provides one of the best opportunities to take a trophy tiger muskellunge. Concentrate on the northern areas of the lake such as off Lader Point and the narrows before the dam, and work the edge of the weeds. Live bait such as golden shiners work best. Jigging lures, like the Rapala with the plastic tail that makes the weighted minnow lure flutter when dropped, would be my second choice. You can expect to catch tigers up to 12 pounds.

When using minnows and shiners, it is important to prevent thermo shock, a sure way to kill your bait. If you can purchase your bait from a dealer with outdoor bait tanks, that is the best. But if not, you need to reduce the temperature in your minnow bucket a little at a time until it nearly matches the water temperature of the lake. Smart ice anglers add a little snow or ice to the bucket as they travel to their favorite fishing hole. If you do not match the lake temperature the sudden shock of being moved from warm tank water to the 39 degree or colder lake water will most likely kill the minnow within minutes. An inexpensive thermometer will help you gauge this change.

When ice fishing, don't overlook the white perch that are so abundant, nor the yellow perch or crappie. The southern waters of the lake, off the causeway, are the most productive areas for this angling. Jigs tipped with spikes, mousie grubs or fathead minnow are the standard choices

Care should be taken on any lake ice, but especially with the ice of Otisco. This lake is first and foremost a reservoir for the City of Syracuse, and the drawdowns can range up to 100 inches. Significant changes in water levels could weaken the ice, either with currents caused by the withdrawal or from the ice being left high and dry. The same changes in the water level also kill weed growth along the shallow areas of the lake, often eliminating important fish habitat.

Chapter 10
FINGER LAKES TRIBUTARIES
by C. Scott Sampson

Experienced anglers hunt for trout in the Finger Lakes tributaries. Hunting trout is much like gunning for big game. But in this case, you are using a rod, a reel and a pair of Polaroid glasses that allow you to see the trout before you present your bait or lure. In many types of fishing you are working blind, based on your knowledge of good holding water. But hunting trout is different. It might be compared to dry fly fishing, when you work to a visible rise form.

In actuality, you will both hunt and fish for trout in the tributaries. But the strongest memories of my success seem to be centered around the "hunted trout."

Homer was a male rainbow of some four pounds that I hunted, caught and released twice before he disappeared. It all happened on a small tributary to Seneca Lake, a miniature Watkins Glen gorge, if you will, that will remain nameless. The stream has both steep rock walls and multiple falls. The falls are not large enough to stop the migration of spawning rainbow trout. But they are large enough to make intermittent pools. In some places, the banks rise nearly 100 feet and periodically a tree will lose its rooting from erosion and topple into the narrow passage, adding structure to the stream.

It was already the second week of the season. (These tributaries open on April 1st.) I was hunting trout and exploring as much as I was fishing. I had followed the stream up from the lake looking for new pools and wondering just how far a trout might go. A smaller branch of the stream broke off to my right and I followed it. Felt soles (I now often wear steel spikes) held me securely on the slate bottom. The sun was already starting to produce the algae cover that greases the rocks and can turn an angler upside down and start him down the currents of hell. There was a section of gently sloped but totally smooth stream bottom with less than an inch of water moving across it. Certainly that would end any possibility of trout. I continued on in hopes of finding a shorter way into the better pools from a road I knew lay just ahead.

You tend to become arrogant when hunting trout in crystal clear water with brown-colored Polaroids. You think you can see everything. There was a log jam ahead. A shadow rolling across the pool caught my attention. A rainbow, that I later named Homer, was cruising. He moved in and out from the edge of a log looking for food, but not willing to remain exposed. The logs had plugged the bottom of the gorge. There were no banks where I could get out of the stream to move ahead and position myself above the fish in such a way that I could drift a spawn sack through the currents he was working.

I could see his red mid-line clearly. He was a mature fish brightly dressed in spawning color. The rest of the body was dark, indicating he had been in the stream at least several days. Even if I spooked him, where would he go? Certainly not downstream; there was not enough water right now. He would have to wait for the next rain to do that.

With my spinning rod I lobbed the spawn over the logs and it landed a foot in front of the fish. I never saw the strike, just the explosion of water as the rainbow attacked the fresh eggs. I scrambled over the log dam like a squirrel, all the time praying I could keep the fish out of the ragged edges of the dam.

I debated killing the fish because he appeared trapped, but he had given me too much pleasure. If nothing else, I could be reasonably assured that he would still be here tomorrow. His lower jaw was just beginning to hook. Homer was a beautiful

and very distinctive fish. I let him go for another day, another challenge.

I had found a shorter way into the special water from upstream. Homer was not as obvious. I carefully searched the pool before seeing a pectoral fin stabilizing a trout holding tight under the same log where Homer had first been seen. Good holding water is always good, and new fish will move into good habitat as soon as it is vacant.

Now I could drift my spawn sack past the fish. My first flip and drift did nothing. I was working an experienced fish. In low clear water, I work the spawn sack without weight. It gives the most natural action, freely rolling with the gentle current with no resistance. My number 6 salmon egg style red finished Gamakatsu hook was almost invisible.

I took a deep breath to relax, and started another drift after waiting a respectable minute for the fish to forget anything it might have heard or seen. This time I started the drift at the very front of the pool, a good 10 feet in front of the fish. I pushed line through my guides to eliminate resistance and give the spawn a free run. The fish moved over almost imperceptibly, but enough that I knew he saw the bait. He did not take. On the third drift I moved the sack closer to the bank, but yet still in the current that would tumble it past the fish.

Perhaps the second drift had said "wake up and smell the bacon," because on the third drift there was no hesitation. It was Homer in all his glory.

When I released Homer the second time, I promised to bring a styrofoam cooler the next time so I could carry him over the dam to the pools below. It wasn't necessary. It rained that evening and Homer was free.

My favorite hunting rod is a 6½ foot graphite spinning model and my reel is loaded with six pound test line. Some good anglers use four pound test. A lot of anglers also use a nine foot fly rod for extra reach and load their fly reel with monofilament line. I find the spinning equipment is better for flip casting, especially when I am trying to get my bait back

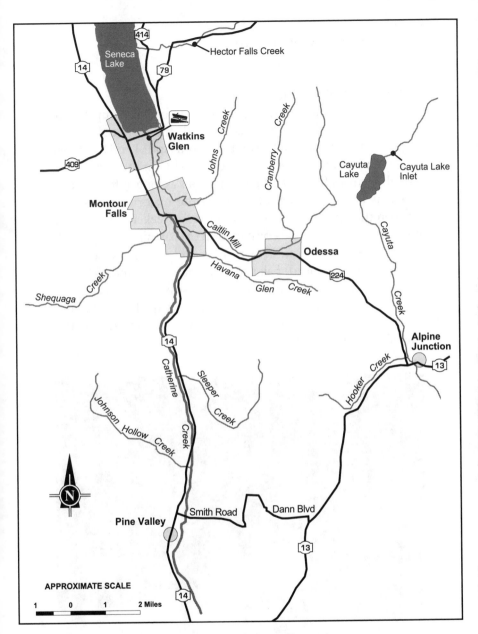

Figure 10.1   Catherine Creek

and under an obstruction.

Angling in the tributaries to the Finger Lakes, up to the first falls impassable by fish, is covered under special fishing regulations. The official season runs from April 1 to December 31, but it is principally a two season activity. In the spring, it is a rainbow trout fishery that generally lasts as long as four weeks. It seems to capture the attention of the majority of anglers only on the opening day and the opening weekend. In the fall, most streams will have a combination of spawning runs including landlocked salmon, brown trout and in some cases rainbow trout or steelhead. Fall runs begin as early as mid-September and continue until the close of the season. Peak activity is often in the first two weeks of October. The quality of the runs in the fall largely depends on the amount of rain. The wetter the fall, the better the runs.

The darkness of this stream-caught rainbow indicates that is has been in the stream for several days. Bright fish, directly from the lake, will begin to darken within hours of entering a tributary.

The principal tributaries for trout and salmon, with the exception of Sugar Creek at Keuka Lake, enter the lakes from the south. Sugar Creek flows south into the northern end of the western fork of Keuka Lake near Branchport.

Catharine Creek feeding Seneca Lake and Naples Creek feeding Canandaigua Lake have in years past enjoyed worldwide reputations for exceptional spring angling. The fishing has not changed much, and if anything, the less crowded conditions today have improved angling opportunity. The fame of yesterday has been lost to the tributaries of Lake Ontario. The excitement of opening day on the Finger Lakes tributaries also has been diluted with the year-round seasons for trout and salmon in both the Finger Lakes proper and the tributaries to Lake Ontario.

Before these changes, April 1st was nearly an official holiday in the Finger Lakes region. Kids and parents both skipped school or work to participate in what has become a rite of spring. Anglers were counted in the tens of thousands. Today, there is still significant interest but with perhaps a 10-fold decrease in the intensity.

The fame of early years was important. It encouraged the DEC to secure an abundance of public access to these waters. The fishing on both Catharine and Naples Creeks is readily accessible. Catharine Creek is 11 miles of trophy water from Pine Valley to Seneca Lake. The primary water is upstream from Montour Falls and runs parallel to Route 414. There is just under seven miles of fishing rights on this stream plus additional public areas on tributaries such as Havana Glen Creek, sometimes called Mitchell Hollow Creek, and Sleeper Creek. Fishermen parking areas are scattered along Route 414.

Naples Creek has 9.5 miles of public access, five parking areas and three foot paths that service anglers. Parking is also available for the stream's more famous sub-tributaries such as Eelpot and Tannery Creeks. You might start your fishing at the junction of Routes 21 and 245 and work your way upstream.

Naples has one of the oldest opening day trout derbies in

the state. It began in 1961. The record winning fish for this water was taken in 1963 by James Grove Sr. and weighed 15 pounds, 5 ounces. The average spring rainbow trout from this water will range in size from three to six pounds. In the fall the fish are slightly smaller.

A similar pattern takes place in Catharine Creek. While there are no records on the largest fish from Catharine, rainbows upward of 14 pounds were taken from here in years past. The fall runs in Catharine Creek also include brown trout. Land-locked salmon is a developing fishery in Seneca Lake and runs of these fish will increase as the species gains a stronger foot-hold in this lake.

The Keuka Outlet drains Keuka Lake into Seneca Lake. In its last 3½ miles before reaching Seneca Lake and after Cascade Mills, the stream offers spawning run angling opportunity in the spring and fall. A warm water discharge from an oil-fired steam generating electric plant is a major attraction for fish at both times of the year.

Some of the best fall spawning runs occur in Cold Brook on Keuka Lake near Hammondsport. This is a relatively short stream at 4.5 miles in length, but it has 3.5 miles of public fishing easements. It is principally spring-fed and has the most consistent flow as well as the best water quality of any tributary to the Finger Lakes. Even after a rain, it remains relatively clear and always fishable. Cold Brook is narrow and deeper than many streams, making the hunting of fish more difficult. But the angling potential is superior.

Cayuga Lake is fed by three principal tributaries: Cayuga Inlet, Fall Creek and Salmon Creek (not to be confused with the Salmon River). Both Salmon and Fall Creeks are relatively short streams, as measured from the lake to the first barrier impassible by fish. They are exciting waters, offering quality angling and an opportunity to take some trophy sized fish. Both have runs of rainbows, browns and landlocked salmon.

The Cayuga Inlet is interrupted by a flood control dam located one mile upstream from the lake. A fish ladder is used to pass the trout and salmon over the dam. Rainbow trout of two to eight pounds make up the bulk of the runs on this stream in the spring and, in the fall, landlocked salmon, originally stocked above the dam, return to spawn. They are in the range of four to six pounds. There are 7.28 miles of public fishing on the Inlet between Buttermilk Creek and West Danby. Angler parking lots are located on Routes 96 and 34.

The angling in Fall Creek is right in the City of Ithaca. Most will concentrate their efforts at the major pool below the falls opposite the high school at Routes 13 and 34. Some of the best fishing on this water is in the fall for landlocks and browns. It is also generally fly fished with streamers. Patterns such as the Fall Favorite, Egg Sucking Leach, Popsicle, Green Butt Skunk and other steelhead or salmon flies are fished more often than the egg or spawn sack.

Salmon Creek has a mile of public water between its mouth on Myers Point and the falls at Ludlowville. It traverses a fast drop to the lake through a series of short, fast riffles that open into some picture perfect pools. Fish can be found holding in any of these pools. This natural design helps to spread out the angling opportunity as compared to Fall Creek, where anglers are in close competition. Salmon Creek is open enough for good fly fishing. I once took about a four pound landlocked salmon on a homemade streamer from this water. The fish leaped, totally clear of the water, seven times before it could be hand-tailed.

Owasco Inlet has 20 miles of trout habitat. It attracts good runs of rainbows in the spring. Browns and a few landlocked salmon use the same water in the fall. Upstream from Moravia to Groton there are resident populations of wild rainbows and browns. There is a total of 13.3 miles of public access on this water. In the lower reaches, just up from the lake, there is a significant warm water fishery for bass and crappie.

Grout Brook is a relatively short stream of six miles that feeds Skaneateles Lake. It has just under two miles of public access and three angler parking areas. Two access areas are on

Glen Haven Road and a third is on Sweeney Hill Road. Grout has both spring and fall runs of salmonids. There are few trophy sized fish, but a good number of 20-inch fish.

Springwater Creek, the feeder and nursery stream for Hemlock Lake, has substantial runs of rainbow in both the spring and fall. But it is difficult to fish because of the overgrown banks. There are public fishing rights from Kellogg Road to Depot Road, and from Kellogg downstream to Hemlock Lake it is open by permit. It is the same permit required to fish Hemlock Lake. The permit is free. See Chapter 8 for details.

Conesus Inlet is an important warm water stream with miles of public assess through the Conesus Inlet Fish and Wildlife Management Area. Tributaries to Honeoye and Otisco lakes are not significant.

The most popular bait for stream run trout and salmon is the spawn sack or eggs. Eggs were made legal for angling in 1976. Previously they were illegal even to possess on a Finger Lake stream. There is little question that eggs are effective, but there are significant differences among eggs of the species they are taken from. There also are differences in the preparation of eggs. The only spawn that can be sold is salmon eggs. Rainbow trout eggs may be used, if you are lucky enough to catch a ripe female. I like to use fresh or untreated eggs when ever possible. I start out with treated eggs but carry a Troy Bait Maker kit in my pocket. The bait maker is a metal sliding system that closes the nylon netting around the eggs. The resulting net bag can then be heat sealed with a lighter flame. It is a method that can be used quickly and easily in the field. The resulting spawn sack should be about the size of your finger nail. Sacks can be made with just eggs or you can add a floater bead of styrofoam to float the spawn off the bottom. The netting used to make the sack also comes in a variety of colors. I prefer the plain eggs and the light pink or yellow netting.

Fresh spawn milks or "bleeds" more readily into the stream current and attracts the trout or salmon. But it is also more fragile than treated eggs, and you will replace the sack after any strike or sometimes just from banging the rock bottom of the stream. Treated eggs are generally toughened by soaking in a solution of boric acid. The treatment is critical. If the eggs are left in the acid solution too long they will become hard, like little rubber balls, and will not be effective. If they are not treated long enough, they will not hold up, and they will begin to rot even under refrigeration.

The standard egg treatment is a solution of three ounces of powdered boric acid dissolved in a quart of water. Soak the eggs in this solution for two hours. Drain and rinse well in fresh water before tying into spawn sacks. Even prepared bait should be refrigerated for longer storage life. Dedicated anglers will change and then carefully guard their formula when they find something that works well for them. Untreated eggs must be refrigerated and will, even then, last only several days before going bad.

While eggs work well, they are not the only bait. Anglers are returning to the use of artificial lures. Spawn balls or egg flies, the colorful, fuzzy, artificial steelhead enticer that gained popularity on Lake Ontario tributaries, are now being used in the Finger Lakes. So are baits that were popular years ago. If you took a survey before the legalization of eggs — say along Catharine or Naples Creeks on opening day — you would have found almost anything. Small sections of sponge imitating spawn was the most popular. This sponge was often saturated with petroleum jelly to which anise oil was added for flavor and smell. Every angler seemed to have a special scent. Corn, jelly beans, marshmallows, cheese balls, bits of potato, hotdogs or anything else you might have for lunch was also used.

The critical factor was then, as it is today, to make the correct presentation of the bait or lure to the fish. That means drifting it at the same speed as the current, and right along the bottom of the stream.

The successful angler is also a cautious angler. He or she makes a careful approach to the stream, wears dark colored clothing, keeps the sun in his face and, above all, works his bait

Head cement is applied to a streamer fly that is of the style and design for fall-run trout and salmon in the Finger Lakes tributaries.

carefully. Be sure to work your offering along and under the bank overhangs as well as in the more obvious fish holding areas.

There are many smaller tributaries to the Finger Lakes that I have not named. They are mostly on private property, and without public easement. Some are seasonal waters, meaning they go dry in the summer, and often depend on drainage ditches for their water flow in the spring. Some are not even a hundred yards long from the lake to the first impassable barrier, but many hold spawning fish and can provide enjoyable angling. Remember to ask permission. Gaining access is generally an easy task, especially if you promise to leave only footprints.

Not all the action in the tributaries is leaping silver. Smelt and suckers run up many of these same waters in the spring of the year. Dipping either of these fish can provide some excellent eating as well as recreation. Taughannock Creek on Cayuga Lake at Taughannock State Park has a less than mediocre trout and salmon run but a good smelt run in the spring. There are other streams of similar reputation but many have significant runs of both.

Smelt and sucker dipping is generally open year around, and around the clock in the tributaries to Canandaigua, Canadice, Hemlock, Keuka and Seneca lakes. There are some exceptions such as Catharine Creek which is closed to dipping. Dipping is controlled on Cayuga and Owasco for diplomatic reasons, specifically to minimize conflicts between anglers and residents. Here the season is open only between March 1 and May 21, and between the hours of 7 p.m. to 2 a.m. All the Finger Lakes waters have an eight quart limit for smelt, and unlimited numbers of suckers may be taken. Check your regulations guide for any changes to these rules and limitations on your particular water.

Dip netting either of these fish is in large measure a social occasion. Gas lanterns are normally used to light the stream while anglers work in teams to drive the fish into a pool or into each other's dip nets. It should be noted that smelt will, at times, run in daylight hours. The better long handled nets have a wire mesh bag that stands up to the abuse of working it over the stream bottom. If you are buying a net, be sure that it has a wooden handle. Metal is just too cold on a spring night. A five gallon bucket is often used to carry the bounty. The handle is run through the angler's belt. The larger bucket allows you to flip the smelt out of your net and into the pail without having to get your hands wet. A smelt angler has his hands filled anyway, with a lantern in one and his net in the other.

Smelt in the Finger Lakes tributaries normally begin to run when the temperature in the stream reaches 48 degrees. That may or may not coincide with the opening of the trout season. The common sucker runs are also triggered by this same water temperature.

Spring suckers are an exceptionally fine eating fish. But, you have to be careful in cooking because of the abundance of bones. Some people fillet the sucker and then grind the fillets for fish cakes. An alternative, and one preferred in the Finger Lakes region, is to first scale the fish, and then cut the fillet off each side. The fillet is laid, skin side down, on a cutting board and the flesh is scored with a knife down to, but not through, the skin every quarter inch. The scored fillets are then dipped in batter and deep fried. The hot fat dissolves the bones. Suckers are some of the best eating fish you can find when they come out of the cold spring waters of the Finger Lakes tributaries.

PART II

OTHER WATERS
OF THE
FINGER LAKES REGION
AND WESTERN NEW YORK

Chapter 11
ONEIDA LAKE
by Leo Maloney

Visualize a 22 mile long fishing hole accessible by major highways and containing over half a million walleyes, lots of smallmouth and largemouth bass, yellow perch and many other gamefish and panfish. That's Oneida Lake.

With angling friend Pat Ray, I've caught bass in the morning, perch in the afternoon and walleye in the evening – all on the same day. It was a marathon of fishing that I don't recommend to everyone but it points out the diverse opportunity on Oneida Lake.

Many people have called Oneida Lake one of the best fishing spots in New York State, and for sheer numbers and variety it would be hard to dispute that label. Walleyes are the local favorite, but the bass and perch also provide top quality fishing. Other popular species include northern pike, catfish, bullhead, crappies, and a variety of panfish.

Oneida Lake is located just north of Syracuse and stretches out 22 miles in an east-west direction. It averages about five miles in width. Most of the lake is relatively shallow, with depths ranging from 20 to 38 feet. The deepest part of the lake is in the east-central portion, where depths range from 40-50 feet.

The area is easily reached via Interstate 81 or 90 (New York State Thruway) in conjunction with State Routes 31, 13, 5, and 49. Several cities and towns border its shore or are within easy driving distance, and these can provide angler support services.

Numerous bait shops, marinas, and restaurants are located along Oneida's shoreline. State boat launching sites on the north shore at Godfrey Point near Cleveland and at Three Mile Bay, west of Constantia, in addition to the Southshore Ramp near Bridgeport afford convenient access. There are dozens of marinas and private facilities around the lake offering launch ramps for a fee, gas, services, and boat rentals.

The Barge Canal is routed through the middle of the lake, and it is marked with buoys. Anglers often use these buoys as reference points. There are piers at the canal entrances at Sylvan Beach on the east end and at Brewerton on the west end; both are popular shore fishing spots.

Many tributaries to the lake also offer good fishing. These include Fish Creek, Oneida Creek, Canaseraga Creek, Chittenango Creek, and Scriba Creek. All these streams experience spawning runs of walleyes in the spring, and contain bass and northern pike all year long.

The Barge Canal, beginning at Sylvan Beach, provides fishing for walleyes, largemouth and smallmouth bass, catfish, and tiger muskies. Spinnerbaits, jigs, and crankbaits all work well along the rocky shores and overhanging willows. The Oneida River, which drains the lake at the west end and is part of the canal system, offers similar fishing opportunities.

The most popular species among Oneida anglers is the walleye, referred to as "pike" by local anglers, and it is easy to see why. Oneida Lake rates among the top walleye waters in the state. Perhaps the top, considering the number of walleye produced. The lake contains an average of 500,000 to 750,000 adult walleyes according to Cornell University research studies.

The lake is managed for numbers, not size, so the walleyes are not as large as those from some other areas of the state. The average walleye will be about one and one-half to three pounds. Anglers should check the current fishing guide for special regulations and size limits because the size limit on Oneida Lake may differ from the tributaries or surrounding waters.

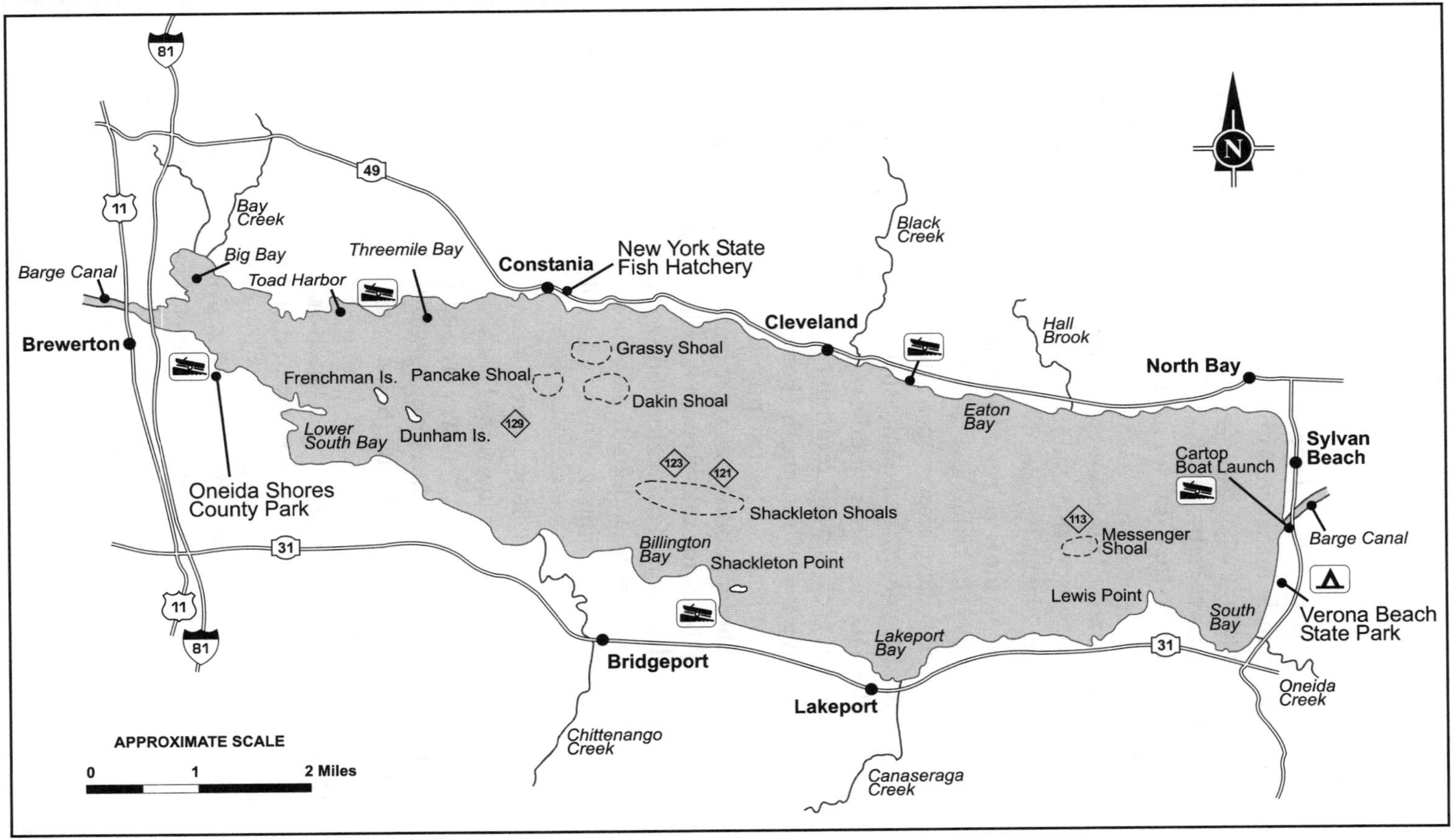

Figure 11.1 Oneida Lake

Walleye are the control species in the lake. That is to say, the population is managed to remain stable and in concert with the available forage base. Cornell University maintains a biological research station at Shackelton Point, and makes recommendations to the DEC for management of the lake's fisheries.

Walleye season lasts from early May through March 15, and provides almost year-round recreation. Fishing from a boat is the most popular and productive way of fishing for walleyes, although wading the shallows and casting to the fish provides action for anglers in spring and fall.

When the walleye season opens the first Saturday in May, anglers tend to concentrate on the shallow areas of the eastern basin of the lake or off the mouths of major tributary streams. Late spawners are often still returning from the creeks and anglers working jigs slowly along the bottom will be successful.

For boat anglers, the most popular method is trolling stickbaits or flutter spoons using flat lines or lead core lines. Popular stickbaits include Rebel, Rapala, Nilsmaster, and Mirrolure. I have found best colors tend to be black and silver, black and gold, green and gold, perch, or red and white. A slow troll with lures running about 75 to 100 feet behind the boat works best.

Other productive techniques in May and June include the worm and spinner rig or jigs tipped with a worm or minnow. Early in the season, when walleyes are still in shallow water, drifting along the edges of the emerging weedbeds with a worm and spinner rig or jigs is effective. Some of my favorite areas are along the north shore from Cleveland to North Bay and on the east end of the lake off Verona Beach State Park.

In June the walleyes move to the deeper water in the eastern and central portions of the lake. Throughout the summer months, the most productive method is trolling the deeper water, 35 to 45 feet, using lead-core line or downriggers. The stickbaits in color combinations mentioned earlier are still the best lures to use. The area between buoys 113 and 121 north of Messenger Shoals and Shackelton Shoals tends to be the most productive.

In early summer and fall, walleyes come into shallow areas to feed on baitfish during the evening hours. At this time many anglers wade out and cast for them with stickbaits. The best areas for wading include Lewis Point, Verona Beach Lighthouse, North Bay, Shackelton Point, and Bernhards Bay. Preference should be given to where the onshore wind is blowing, since the wind can bring in the baitfish and the walleyes that follow them.

Anglers who want large walleyes should concentrate on the deeper water, even in the early season. Pat Roy and I broke the tradition of shallow water walleye fishing one day. We headed for the deep water off Shackelton Shoals, even though we saw shallow water anglers taking 15 to 17 inch walleye one after another. We worked jigging spoons and jigs tipped with nightcrawlers in 20 to 30 feet of water to take limits of walleyes that ranged from 20 to 23 inches in length. Work your baits very slowly.

The type and color of jigging spoon usually depends on the angler's preference or what seems to be working best that day. Some popular types of jigging spoons are the Bomber Slab Spoon, Cordell CC Spoon, Mepps #1 Syclops, and Heddon Sonar model 431. Proven colors are silver, gold, white, natural perch, chartreuse, and hot orange.

One of the most successful Oneida Lake guides is Captain Tony Buffa. His favorite method is drifting whenever there is a northwest wind and a two foot wave chop. During these conditions walleyes will often be suspended, especially around the shoals in the center of the lake.

Buffa suggests using a number four or six gold plated hook tied directly to a four foot leader of six pound Trilene XL line. This leader is connected to a three way swivel at the end of six pound test line. The third swivel connection supports a six-inch dropper with enough weight to bring the bait within half or two-thirds of the depth of water in that area.

Run this rig at least 100 feet behind your boat. The exact length of line and amount of weight will depend on wind speed and depth of water. Buffa free-spools to the bottom every few minutes and then takes up a couple turns on the reel. He does this until he either catches a walleye or no longer can reach bottom. At that time he reels in and starts the drift over.

The key to successful walleye fishing is to present a nightcrawler or minnow in a very natural way. Don't curl the worm on the hook. Place no more than one half inch of the worm on the hook shank to keep it natural. Too much weight will make a bait appear sluggish and cause too much resistance upon contact with a walleye, not to mention lots of snags.

Buffa's method of drifting works well throughout most of the lake. Some of the most productive areas for drifting are in the vicinity of Messenger Shoals, northwest of Lewis Point, Shackelton Shoals, north of Shackelton Point, and the various shoals south of Constantia.

Bass are often referred to as the forgotten fish in Oneida Lake because of the popularity of walleyes. This lake does offer some very good fishing for both largemouth and smallmouth bass.

When the season opens on the third Saturday in June, the best bet is to try for them along the shoals near shore. The lake has lots of weedbeds and shoals, and these make good bass habitat. As the summer progresses, concentrate in the deeper water along these areas during the day and fish slightly shallower during the evening.

If there is a gentle wind blowing from the west or northwest try drifting with worms, minnows or softshell crabs on a number six gold hook tied directly to six pound test line. If there is no wind, anchor at a point where the weeds meet the rocky structure and present the bait in a vertical manner. Use split shot about six inches above the bait.

These same junctures of weeds and rocky structure are also good places to cast with crankbaits, stickbaits, jigs, or spinners. Crankbaits in shad or crawfish patterns such as the Rebel Double Deep Shad are usually very effective.

Some of the best spots for smallmouth bass include the bars and shoals near Lewis Point, Shackelton Point, Bernhards Bay, Messenger Bay, Eaton Bay, and around Frenchman and Dunham Islands.

Largemouth bass are found in most of the larger bays that contain weeds or grassy areas. Good spots to try for largemouths include South Bay, North Bay, Lakeport Bay, Lower South Bay, Big Bay, Toad Harbor, and Three Mile Bay.

Because these areas are also likely to see a lot of boat traffic the best time to fish for bass is early in the morning. Pat Roy, a bass pro and fishing guide, suggests that one should first go after the active fish by casting large spinnerbaits, crankbaits, or Mepps style spinners over the weeds or through the openings. If that doesn't produce, switch to plastic worms or jigs and carefully work these back through the openings of the weedbeds.

Live bait such as crabs or minnows, fished in or along the weeds, also yield good results. Hook crabs through the mid-tail section, and hook minnows through the lips; add one or two split shot for weight.

Most bays are relatively shallow and without any significant drop-offs. Look for subtle changes in structure and cover. In addition to fishing the edges of weedbeds, look for any changes in weed types or cover. In summer, look for the darkest water you can find. In the fall, fish the clearest water.

Large yellow perch, referred to locally as jack perch, keep anglers busy when the bass or walleyes aren't cooperating. These perch often run as large as 12-14 inches, and are found throughout the lake along the weedbeds or the edges of shoals. As the water warms in summer, the perch will be found in deeper water off the same structure.

Casting over the weedbeds with small spinners or one-eighth ounce bucktail jigs in brown, black, white, or yellow is a good way to locate perch. Fishing live bait such as softshell crabs, worms, or small minnows along the weeds is another productive method.

There is a wide variety of other fish inhabiting the lake and offering surprises or action for the angler. These include silver bass, white perch, carp, crappies, bullhead, catfish, northern pike and an occasional tiger musky. Spring is naturally the best time for bullhead. Fishing with worms all along the shore, especially by the mouths of creeks, can sometimes yield bullheads by the pailful.

Northern pike are not really numerous because much of their prime spawning habitat of shallow swamp-like bays has been destroyed by shoreline development. However, some pike can be found in the weedy bays along shore, and some large ones (5-10 lbs.) are caught every year. One good method is to fish live minnows. Another is to cast spinners, spinnerbaits, or stickbaits over or around the weedbeds.

Ice fishing is almost as popular as summer fishing on Oneida Lake. Weekends in winter find hundreds of anglers scattered across the ice in search of perch and walleye. Both tip-ups and jigging rods are used.

Ice tends to form at the eastern end of the lake and in the shallow bays first. Local anglers agree that "early ice" is best for walleye fishing. When the lake first freezes over in late December or early January, the walleyes will be found in relatively shallow water, often eight to fifteen feet. By late January or February the walleyes will be deeper, in over 28 feet of water, and the action will be much slower. Ice fishermen move further offshore and more toward the west as the season progresses.

Preparations for mid-lake ice fishing are often elaborate. Because of the openness, protection from the weather in the form of ice shanties or canvas shelters such as dome tents is often used. Snowmobiles and ATVs are the norm for mid-lake fishing. Unfortunately, while as much as 18 inches of ice may accumulate in some years, nearly every year someone using an RV breaks through the ice. Extreme caution should be observed at all times when taking a vehicle on the ice.

In a good winter, semi-permanent ice shanty cities spring up at mid-lake. Anglers may leave their structures on the ice but they must be identified with the owner's name and address and removed from the ice before the thaw. Leaving a shanty in place, even one on skids, saves a considerable amount of fishing time. When the ice is good, guided ice fishing will be available; of course when you hire such a service you get to use their shanty.

Jigging is the most common ice fishing technique for perch and walleyes. The best method is to find the bottom, come up 18-24 inches, jig lightly and hold it still for a while before you jig again. Popular brands of jigging lures are gold or silver Sidewinders, Swedish Pimples, Kastmasters, or Super Dupers. Many anglers like to add a perch eye, or a one-quarter-inch strip of fish meat to the hook.

Perch fishermen should use tackle no heavier than four pound test line and number eight treble hooks on the lure, regardless of lure size. Put a split ring on top of the lure and tie that to the line. Use short, sharp jigging movements, moving the rod no more than two or three inches. Later in the season tear drop jigs with mousie grubs seem to work better for perch.

Under early ice, the perch are also found in shallow water, usually 12 to 18 feet. But after mid-January one usually has to work his way out over deeper water to find them. The general advice is to keep moving until perch are found. If there is no action after 15 minutes or so, move on and cut some more holes.

Periods of low light, such as early morning or late afternoon, are generally best for walleyes and crappies. By mid-winter, when the action is usually in the middle of the lake, anglers will have to travel a long way unless they go out from a point of land such as Lewis or Shackelton Points. Just in case snow or fog sets in, it's essential to carry a compass to find one's way back.

Check ice depth and conditions before venturing out on the ice. The areas around the mouths of creeks may have dangerously thin ice. Winds whipping the length of the lake can often drop the wind chill factor to minus 10 or 20 degrees, so it is important to dress warmly.

Many restaurants and bait shops around the lake remain open in the winter and cater to ice fishermen. Parking and access is available from the state boat launch areas or many bait shops. Check with bait shops or local anglers to see where the best action is and what the fish are biting on.

Chapter 12
THE FIVE BEST STREAMS
IN DEC REGION 7
by J. Michael Kelly

C azenovia resident Tony Dennison was the toast of Syracuse newspaper outdoor columnists in the 1960s and early '70s because of his ability to fill sports-page holes with "big trout" pictures. In those days before Lake Ontario was blaanketed with charter boats and planer boards, a five-pound brown trout was a rarity in most New York waters. But Dennison landed several each season from local trout streams. Some of his most impressive trophies, browns with pot bellies and gnarly jaws, came from Fabius Brook.

Fabius is a cross between a dream and a nightmare. Anglers who take the time to study the brook soon understand its potential for holding some beautiful fish, but wonder how they can possibly catch them. From its swampy beginnings to its confluence with the West Branch of Tioughnioga Creek, Fabius is a nine-mile-long obstacle course better suited to gung-ho Marines than casual fishermen. Be forewarned, you'll have to climb over deadfalls, wade through boggy pastures and poke your rod tip through curtains of alders if you want to shake hands with the residents of Fabius Brook.

Is it worth the trouble? You bet. Dennison swears the 10 pounder he caught below Parker Road was dwarfed by a bigger Fabius Brook brown trout, and retired DEC Region 7 fisheries biologist Cliff Creech says his electroshocking crews turned up 18 inch brookies in the stream. Newcomers can't realistically hope for such fish, but wild brookies of eight to 10 inches and foot-long browns are routine. And a much bigger fish is always possible.

Fly fishermen are frustrated by Fabius Brook's thick bank cover and clear, smooth currents. Yet the stream has good hatches of Light Hendrickson mayflies in May and June, followed by summer emergences of tiny blue-winged olives (size 20) and *Tricorythodes* (size 22 or 24). An assortment of tan and olive-bodied caddis flies come off the water, too. However, dry fly fishing is difficult in these confined quarters and you'll do better by roll casting weighted nymphs, particularly a size 14 Hendrickson or a size 12 Peeking Caddis, through the deep pools and riffles.

Fabius is better bait water, frankly. Dennison threads minnows on a double hook, while I've had nice catches on small garden worms, particularly after a spring shower has added a little color to the water. Look closely at a map when you make your first visit to Fabius. It's formed by two main branches. One, populated mainly by brook trout, winds from west to east along county Route 80 to the village of Fabius. The other, more productive and holding numerous nice browns, bubbles out of a cedar and alder swamp north of Fabius, then parallels Route 91 to the village. The branches, both crossed by country roads, are less than 10 feet wide in most places. Below their junction near Fabius Junior-Senior High School, you'll find the brook's deepest, widest pools, including a couple of hat-floaters.

The DEC has acquired 1.4 miles of public fishing rights on Fabius Brook along Keeney Road. Much of the rest of the stream is posted, but the dairy farmers who own the adjacent land are uniformly friendly and inclined to grant permission to any angler daring enough to plunge into the thickets.

ORISKANY CREEK

I introduced fly fisherman Bruce Douglas to Oriskany Creek

one muggy June evening when the mosquitoes and deer flies were having a "torment the humans" contest. It wasn't exactly love at first sight.

The creek had a milky tinge after two days of showers, and by the time the sun was touching the hills that surround the Madison County hamlet of Solsville, we'd caught just three small trout.

Then somebody flipped a switch.

While we watched in amazement, hundreds and hundreds of mayflies, sulfur-colored pale evening duns, began to pop through the surface. As the duns fluttered over the stream, trout began to rise with audible blips.

In the next 15 minutes, Bruce and Oriskany Creek became fast friends. The browns we caught weren't big, but they were etched in bright yellows and reds and tugged fiercely when they felt the sting of our size 16 dry fly hooks.

Local anglers make regular visits to Oriskany, and the DEC has assured its continuing popularity with the acquisition of

Oriskany Creek provides pleasant hours astream for the trout fisherman. This shot was taken just upstream of Oriskany Falls.

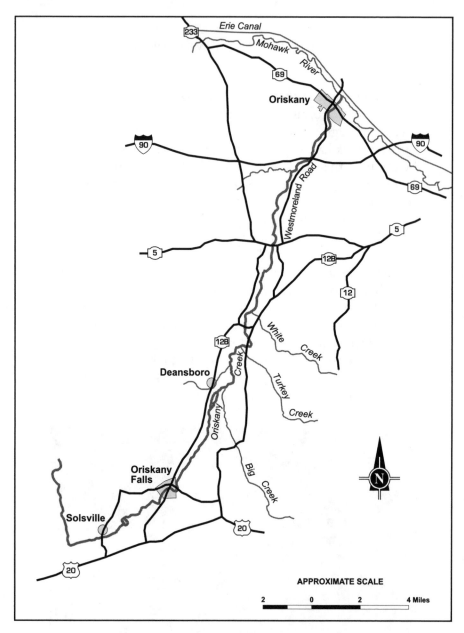

Figure 12.1   Oriskany Creek

14.5 miles of public fishing easements on its approximately 22 mile length.

This creek is almost three streams in one. From the headwaters above Solsville to the Deansboro area across the border in Oneida County, Oriskany Creek isn't stocked, but has thousands of wild browns in its little riffles and meadow bends. Here the creek is less than 15 feet wide in most places, but there are some pools deep enough to hide a few 12 to 14 inchers. From Deansboro to Clark Mills, the fish are bigger, with a few two pound holdovers hiding in some of the deeper, aldershrouded holes. But the wild trout of the upper reaches are gradually supplanted by stocked browns. Finally, from Clark Mills to Oriskany, where the creek spills into the Mohawk River, anglers encounter what DEC aquatic biologist Jack Hasse calls "the transition zone." In this section, where the creek flattens out and some pools are more than 100 feet across, anglers are more apt to catch a smallmouth bass, rock bass or chub than a trout — but the trout caught here are the biggest in the watershed. Three pounders are common, Hasse said.

Oriskany is stocked in its middle and lower reaches with more than 8,000 yearling browns in the spring and spiced with 700-plus 2 year olds of 14 inches. Paralleled by County Route 43 in Madison County and Routes 12B and 32 in Oneida County, it receives moderate to heavy angling pressure in April, May and June, but is lightly fished from then until the regular season closes September 30. From the College Street bridge in Clinton downstream to its meeting with the Mohawk, Oriskany is open until November 30, and fishermen are allowed to keep 5 trout of any size. However, few anglers take advantage of this late season opportunity.

The creek is a worm-dunker's paradise after a quick summer rain shower, but it's treasured by area fly casters because of the heavy mayfly hatches that occur from mid-May into July.

The pale evening dun, or sulfur, emerges for about four weeks starting in the last week of May. There are good hatches of March browns about June 1-10, followed a few days later by the emergence of *Ephemera varia*, the yellow drake. This big mayfly is best imitated by a size 10 cream-bodied dry and closely resembles the famed green drake spinner, or coffin fly, both in appearance and behavior. The action occurs late in the evening from mid-June until about the fourth of July, and anglers who stay until dark may be shocked by the size of some of the browns that greet *varia*.

Although the lower reaches of Oriskany Creek are marginally warm in mid-summer, the sections just downstream from Solsville stay cool year-round and are worth fishing even in late July or early August, given normal rainfall. Early risers may find trout rising to tiny (size 24) *Tricorythodes* mayflies in July and August, and dog-day anglers can always pick up a few pan-sized browns on live grasshoppers or their imitations.

SKANEATELES CREEK

Newcomers to Skaneateles Creek are pleasantly surprised by the quality of fishing in this little stream. It has both wild and stocked brown trout, plentiful stocked rainbows, and some of the best mayfly hatches in Central New York. But to veteran anglers and long-time residents of the creek valley, the most amazing thing about Skaneateles Creek is that it has any fishing at all.

In 1969, a local conservation officer sank a wire basket full of minnows into the creek and eyed his stopwatch. All the minnows died within 60 seconds. Skaneateles Creek was so polluted that no fish could live in it. For more than 100 years, furniture and paper mills, chemical plants, cheese factories and municipal sewers had spewed organic wastes into the 13-mile creek. At times, pH readings rose from the stream's natural level of 7 to as high as 11. That's roughly as alkaline as lye.

The 1970s brought a dramatic turnaround in water quality as tougher state and federal pollution statutes shut off effluent sources, one by one. As pH levels fell and oxygen levels rose, the DEC authorized annual stockings of more than 5,000 trout by Onondaga County's Carpenter's Brook Fish Hatchery. Nonetheless, trout tissue samples taken in 1992 did show some

This Skaneateles Creek brown accepted a small spoon that was cast upstream and brought back just faster than the current.

PCB contamination. Because of the contamination, the first 10 miles of the stream from the Old Seneca Turnpike Bridge to Jordon is a no-kill catch and release water only.

Today Skaneateles is classified as a C(t) stream — capable of supporting trout — for its entire length, and fishing is good from the lake outlet dam in downtown Skaneateles all the way to the creek's confluence with the Seneca River north of Jordan.

There are no state public fishing easements on Skaneateles, but few posted signs dot its banks and most property owners welcome polite fishermen. The stream is just 20 minutes from downtown Auburn via Route 5, and it is crisscrossed by 18 county and town roads. In spite of this accessibility, the creek receives only moderate angler pressure after the first two or three weeks of the trout season have passed.

Fishing is dependably good in Skaneateles Creek from opening day until about the second week of July, when rising water temperatures usually force most of the holdover trout to migrate to a few scattered spring holes.

With an abundance of mayflies and caddis and a huge population of dace, chubs and baby Suckers, the creek is able to feed some oversized trout, and each season brings news of a couple of four-pounders. My personal best is a 21 inch brown that grabbed a dead-drifted garden worm in a Jordan pool. But Syracuse resident Dean White topped that with a 24 incher the next opening day.

Skaneateles Creek averages barely 15 feet wide and a foot deep, and has few holes that will fill your hip boots. That makes locating fish relatively easy, but also puts a premium on stealth and a quiet approach. Bait fishermen who walk quietly and wade as little as possible will often be rewarded with limit catches of 9 to 12 inch browns and rainbows when the creek is roiled after a spring shower. And spin fishermen can fill their creels by using ultralight rigs and tiny Panther Martin, Mepps or Hildebrandt Flicker spinners.

Yet this stream is best-suited to the fly fisher. Some of the prettiest dry fly water in the region can be found on the stretches near Skaneateles Falls and along Route 31C between Elbridge and Jordan. The stream is narrow and tree-lined, and casts are often of the side-arm lob variety, but the action is hot, particularly when the sulfurs — *Ephemerella rotunda* and *Ephemerella dorothea* — hatch from mid-May through mid-June. On a humid evening, it's possible to catch a dozen or more browns and rainbows, including some that are a foot long or better on sulfur patterns. I like size 14 and 16 pale yellow comparaduns and rusty poly-wing spinners.

Skaneateles Creek also has dependable hatches of March browns in early June and sporadic emergences of many caddis species from late April through July.

While Skaneateles Creek trout are sluggish and hard to catch during the heat of summer, fishing picks up after Labor Day. That may be the best time of all to connect with a lunker brown. Try using a live sucker minnow, a spinner or perhaps a slowly twitched brown bucktail.

CHENANGO RIVER

When God created the Chenango River, he must have had canoe trips in mind. This placid stream is tailor-made for anglers

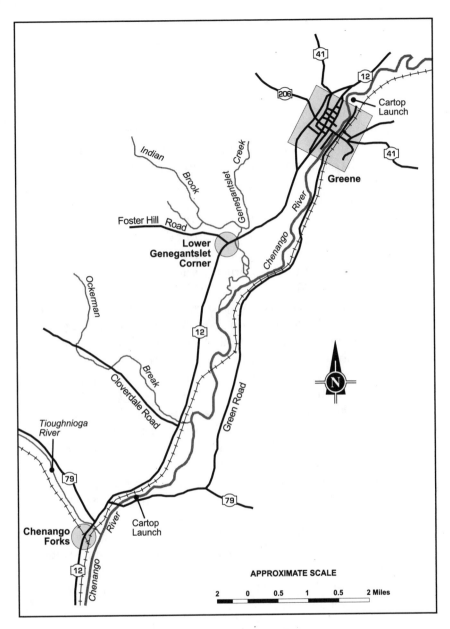

Figure 12.2 Chenango River

who like to float to their fishing holes. The 10 mile stretch from Green to Chenango Forks is just short enough to be covered in a long day by two strong paddlers, and is loaded with smallmouth bass, walleyes and northern pike. The trip contains no hazards, no portage of more than a hundred feet or so, and is well suited to beginning canoeists. Anglers who make the journey will enjoy a rare solitude as well, since there are no road crossings and only a handful of river-bank homes between the launch site at the Green Fairgrounds and the take-out at the Chenango Forks marina and campground.

Although the river is normally safe and enjoyable to float from about mid-May to November, I'd recommend a day trip in July or August as a great way to beat the summer heat. It's a good idea to check ahead on river conditions by calling the DEC Region 7 office in Cortland, but assuming river conditions are normal, you're in for a pleasant trip.

After leaving one car at the aforementioned campground, just north of the intersection of Routes 79 and 12 in Broome County, take a 10 minute drive back up Route 12 to Greene. Turn right (east) onto Route 206, then turn into the Greene Fairgrounds immediately before the bridge over the river. Lower your canoe into the river and shove off.

The first good hole is just downstream off the Route 206 bridge, and the old trestle pool just below that is a real dandy for bass or walleyes. But don't tarry too long; there's almost 10 miles to go. Other notable fish hangouts include a lazy bend adjacent to the Greene Airport, a series of riffles and islands above and below Genegantslet Creek, and a railroad trestle that spans the river about two-thirds of the way to Chenango Forks.

Turn over a few rocks on the stream bed and you'll realize one of the secrets to catching Chenango River bass. The river is a crayfish factory. While there's nothing quite like the real thing, any lure that imitates crayfish — brown or olive jigs, deep diving crankbaits and the like — will put bass on the stringer. The jigs will pull in the walleyes, too. For northerns, or the rare tiger muskellunge that occasionally shocks a

Chenango fisherman, a spoon or bucktail spinner would be a better choice. The Chenango has an abundance of fallfish up to 15 inches long (you'll think you've got a dandy smallmouth when one picks up your softshell crayfish), and they often wind up in the stomachs of big pike or tiger muskies.

Anglers can reasonably hope for a two or three pound smallmouth if the bass are biting during their float, although the Chenango's smallies average around a pound. Walleyes typically run 14 to 18 inches, but lunkers of five or six pounds turn up now and then. While northerns aren't as common as bass or walleyes here, they often run five pounds or bigger. If you catch a tiger musky, odds are it will be a whopper. The river has produced a couple of 20 pounders in recent summers.

Rock bass, bullheads and sunfish are scattered throughout the river. But if you try for them with a drifted nightcrawler, hang on tight, because you're just as likely to connect with a potbellied carp. The Chenango's shallows are full of them, 10 to 20 pounders that send up spurts of mud as they root along the bottom.

A word of caution about this trip. The last mile or so to the campground take-out point is channelized and wide enough, at about 200 feet, to attract speedboats and water skiers on weekends. Not all of the boaters are considerate of canoeists. It's a good idea to hug the bank or, better yet, affix a small electric motor to your canoe while you negotiate the homestretch.

The Broome County Department of Parks and Recreation offers a detailed map of this and nine other canoe trips in the Binghamton area. You can obtain a copy by writing the department at the Broome County Office Building, Government Plaza, P.O. Box 1766, Binghamton, New York 13902. Expect to pay a nominal fee.

SUSQUEHANNA RIVER

If you're used to trout fishing in brooks and plucking panfish from weedy farm ponds, you might be a bit intimidated when you get your first peek at the Susquehanna River. You needn't be, though. Despite its width of 250 to 1,000 feet, it's a friendly stream, full of well defined pools and riffles and holding plenty of bass, walleyes, muskies and catfish to make you feel at home. To tame this river, don't focus on its 444 mile total length or even the 30 odd miles between Binghamton and Nichols. Instead, pick out a few highly recommended pools and visit them again and again until they're as familiar as a backyard pond.

Rock Bottom Dam is a good place to start. The low dam, upstream from the Exchange Street bridge in Binghamton, digs a plunge pool that's full of scrappy (albeit mostly sub-legal) smallmouth bass and 12 to 16 inch walleyes in mid-summer. Local kids catch buckets full of them, as well as lots of rock bass, on the crayfish and hellgramites they collect from beneath river-bottom rocks. In May and again in November through January, the pools below the dam harbor walleyes that migrate from holes downriver. Some of these weigh six to eight pounds, and can be caught on green or black Mr. Twister jigs, shallow running plugs or drifted nightcrawlers. Above the dam is a long, languid flat that harbors walleyes, bass, an occasional channel catfish and some humongous carp.

The Goudy Station hydro dam a few miles downstream in Johnson City is another hotspot.

Doug Stang, leader of the DEC's warm water unit in Albany, spent many hours assaying the fish populations of the Susquehanna while stationed at the Region 7 DEC office in Cortland. He rates Goudy as one of the best fishing holes in the Southern Tier for smallmouths, walleyes and channel cats. The cats average three to five pounds and will hit diving crankbaits, chartreuse or black jigs and live nightcrawlers as readily as commercial or homemade stinkbaits.

Stang also mentions the area around Murphy's Island, downstream of Goudy Station, for walleyes in spring, fall and through the winter ice. The island area also holds some wild muskellunge and stocked tiger muskies. While the Susquehanna as a whole is a wide, shallow river, the narrower reaches around the islands sometimes plunge to depths of 20 feet or more, Stang pointed out.

In Tioga County, smallmouth bass opportunities abound, particularly in the pools around Hiawatha Island, in the village of Owego and on the sharp river bend upstream from the mouth of Wappasening Creek at Nichols. Walleye fishing is also excellent between Hiawatha Island and Owego, and tiger muskies of up to 20 pounds have been caught in the same stretch.

Stang says there's a clear-cut pattern for finding fish in the Susquehanna. Typically, the smallmouths congregate near the riffly heads of pools, while walleyes school in the deeper, slower portions and in the tail-outs. Muskies and tiger muskies seem to frequent the deepest pools, around sunken trees and other structure.

Access to the Susquehanna is relatively easy, although the DEC hopes to expand boat launch facilities in the Binghamton-Johnson City section.

The Rock Bottom dam area can be fished by shore anglers who park off Riverside Drive. Canoes can also be used to fish the flat upstream and the several nice pools above and below

The Susquehanna River in Binghamton just above Exchange Street. There is plenty of water and excellent bass and walleye fishing here.

the Exchange Street bridge, providing water levels are normal. Cartop boats can be carried to the water at Grippen Park in Binghamton, off Grippen Avenue; at Sandy Beach, off Route 7; or at William H. Hill Park behind Westover Plaza. In the Owego to Nichols stretch, there are several bridge crossings over the river on Routes 17 and 17C and three public boat launches: at Hickories Park just east of Owego, on East River Drive upstream from Nichols, and on West River Drive four miles west of Nichols.

Newcomers to the Susquehanna shouldn't be without a great map. "Your Guide to Broome County Rivers" is available for a nominal fee from the Broome County Department of Parks and Recreation, Box 1766, Government Plaza, Binghamton, NY 13902. Aimed at canoeists, the map pinpoints access points, hazards and take-out places that will be just as helpful to anglers.

Chapter 13
THE FIVE BEST PONDS/LAKES IN DEC REGION 7
by J. Michael Kelly

Y ou'd better wear a smile and bring along a few good
fish stories if you come to Whitney Point Reservoir
in January. It's one of the outstanding ice fishing holes
in New York, and anglers come from distant points to try for a
bucketful of its white crappies.

The reservoir, located along Route 26 just north of the
Broome County village of Whitney Point, was formed in 1942
when the Army Corps of Engineers dammed the lower Otselic
River as a flood control measure. It was later stocked with large
and smallmouth bass, walleyed pike, northern pike, bluegills,
tiger muskellunge, channel cats and striped bass/white bass
hybrids. Oddly enough, the fish that eventually emerged as the
dominant species, the white crappie, never made the stocking
list.

How the crappies came to Whitney Point the DEC can't
say, but no one's complaining. Anglers who locate a school of
them can often boat their 25 fish limit before the action stops,
and a good percentage of these fish will be "slabs" of nine to
11 inches. A daily limit of 25 Whitney Point crappies will feed
a family of four, with leftovers.

Crappies aren't the only fish in the reservoir, of course.
The 4,000-acre lake holds largemouth bass up to five pounds
and has fair fishing for yellow perch. The state-record brown

Whitney Point Reservoir is one of the more popular ice fishing desinations in DEC Region 7. White crappies, shown here with yellow perch, are a big part of the lake's appeal.

bullhead of 3 pounds, 6.25 ounces, was caught here by local angler Duane F. Briggs Jr. in May 1990. Northern pike and walleye aren't common, but tend to run big. And the "whiterock" hybrids, showing up with increased frequency in angler catches, run up to 20 inches. Norlunge or tiger muskies are caught only on rare occasions.

Still, the crappie is king at the Point, and winter is the best time to catch him.

For a real taste of Whitney Point's potential, first-timers should consider signing up for the ice fishing derby sponsored each winter by the Whitney Point Sportsmen's Association. Usually held on the second Saturday in February, it draws about 2,000 fishermen. Between spoonfuls of chili and sips of coffee, they catch thousands of crappies. The biggest is usually more than 14 inches long, and one angler in a past derby stacked up

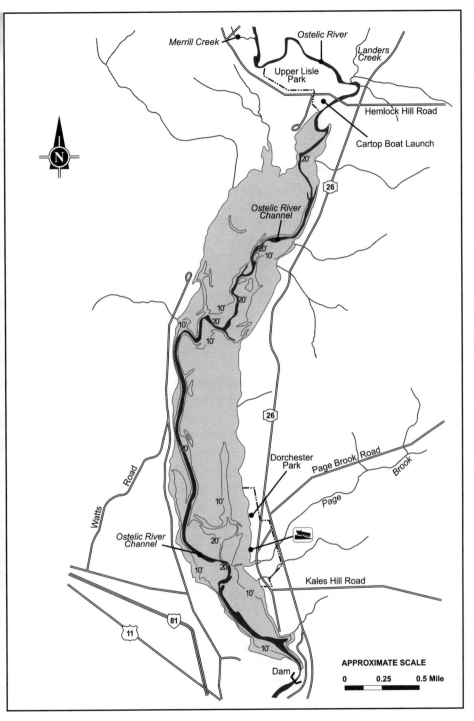

Figure 13.1   Whitney Point Reservoir

309 fish. That was before (and perhaps the reason why) DEC set a 25-fish limit in 1990.

Small shiners are the favorite bait. Experts like Bill Stasko of Endicott puts a one inch "pinhead" shiner on a size 8 hook or teardrop jig, then adds a tiny bobber, and starts reeling as soon as the bobber moves across the hole. Light lines help, and remember that crappies are notoriously soft biters.

Figuring out where to fish is no problem if you're sociable. The crowds will tell you where the action is. On those rare days when you have the ice to yourself, look for branches protruding from frozen-over holes. They're markers left by regulars who have had some success lately.

In May, you can locate spawning schools of crappie in the reservoir's bays and weedbeds. Concentrate on depths of 10 feet or so.

The old Otselic River bed contains some of the best fish-holding structure on the lake, for bass and walleyes as well as crappies. Generally, the channel follows the west shore on the lower half of the reservoir, then takes a sharp right-angle bend at mid-lake. It hugs the east shore the rest of the way to the north end.

Anglers visiting Whitney Point shouldn't overlook the Otselic River immediately downstream of the reservoir spillway. It provides excellent fishing for walleye from about mid-October until the season closes in mid-March. Most of the walleyes are in the 15 to 18 inch range, but some up to eight pounds are taken each year using chartreuse or motor oil Mr. Twister jigs or live red-tail minnows suspended with a bobber.

To reach the reservoir, take the Whitney Point exit off I-81, go east across the bridge in town, then turn north (left) onto Route 26. There are public boat launches and campsites at Dorchester Park on the southeast shore and at Upper Lisle Park at the north end.

If you're driving a long distance and want to check out ice conditions before making the trip, call the Region 7 DEC office at Cortland. The biologists usually keep close tabs on Whitney Point because of its popularity with anglers in the region.

TULLY LAKE

Structure fishermen's eyes light up when they see a topographical map of Tully Lake. Although it's barely 230 acres in size, the lake has a maximum depth of 34 feet, five major points, six glacial kettle basins, numerous steep drop-offs, extensive shallow water weedbeds and an unusual island of emergent cattails and bulrushes in its center. It's hard to find a part of this lake that doesn't look fishy.

Work the drop-offs or the weedbed edges with a grape-colored plastic worm or a black and copper spinnerbait and you may connect with a lunker largemouth. Retrieve a Dardevle or a green and orange Rat-L-Trap over the weed beds and you're apt to bring a four pound pickerel along for the ride. Les Wedge, retired chief of fisheries for DEC Region 7, rates Tully Lake as

Cartoppers and canoes only may be put in at the state launch off Friendly Shore Drive on Tully Lake.

possibly the best spot in the Syracuse area for big largemouths and says it's definitely the premier pickerel pond in Central New York.

"There are good numbers of two to three pound pickerel in the lake, and some even bigger than that," Wedge said. "And it is one of the best bass spots around, too."

In fact, during a three year DEC study of bass angling success on 11 New York lakes and the St. Lawrence River during the late 1970s, the biggest largemouth reported by anglers taking part in the survey came from Tully Lake. It was 27 inches long. Although Wedge has no record of that fish's weight, he's confident it exceeded 10 pounds.

Bill Lang, a real estate agent from Marcellus, and angling buddy Dave Arnold of Camillus have caught many nice bass and pickerel up to five pounds in Tully Lake, but rate it highest as a panfish haven, particularly in the winter months. The pair like the first ice that forms in late December or early January. As soon as the ice is about four inches thick, they drill holes and start jigging with two to four pound-test leaders and tiny hair jigs tipped with mousie grubs. Concentrating on shallows off the boat launch area on Friendly Shores Drive and the aforementioned vegetation island, they sometimes catch 50 or more platter-size bluegills, as well as several nice pickerel in an afternoon of fishing. Now and then they run into a school of large perch, potbellied jacks that are laden with eggs and which stretch out to 12 or 14 inches.

Anglers who prefer pickerel through the ice should augment those jig and grub tactics by rigging a couple of tip-ups with 10 pound leaders and large shiners, preferably the golden shiners that inhabit the lake.

Wedge says shiners and immature bluegills are the primary forage for Tully Lake's bass and pickerel. The predation keeps down panfish numbers but increases their average size. Ten inch bluegills and pumpkinseeds are surprisingly common in the lake.

When the bluegills spawn in early May, Lang reels in fish after fish using a jig tipped with a half-inch piece of nightcrawler or perhaps an oakleaf grub (cranefly larva). He puts a pencil bobber on his line about two or three feet above the hook and adds a small split shot to make the bobber sit up straight. He casts into six feet of water or less, then retrieves slowly, setting the hook whenever the bobber dives.

Although Tully Lake is ringed by camps, its fish aren't overly disturbed by water skiers or swimmers, and fishing can be good throughout the day even in mid-summer.

Access to the Friendly Shores Drive launch area is via Saulsbeery Road in Cortland County or Wetmore Drive in Onondaga County. The DEC maintains a small parking area at the end of Friendly Shores. Anglers are allowed to trailer their boats to the parking area, but must launch by hand, and motor size is limited to 7.5 horsepower or less. In view of those rules, a cartop pram or even a canoe is an excellent choice for exploring Tully Lake.

LITTLE YORK LAKE and GOODALE LAKE

Former Syracuse Herald-Journal Outdoors Editor Fred David is never happier than when he's dragging a plastic frog or Timber King spoon across the matted top of a bass-infested weed bed.

Les Wedge, retired chief of fisheries for Region 7, loves to troll with downriggers for lunker brown trout.

Both anglers find what they're looking for in the same fishing hole: 150 acre Little York Lake in northern Cortland County. David has yanked six pound largemouths from the thick coontail and lilypads that ring the shallows of Little York and Goodale Lakes. Goodale is a 45 acre pond that's separated from Little York Lake by a 10 foot wide channel and the bustling traffic of Interstate 81. Wedge once reeled a six pound brown from the depths of Little York, and says there are bigger ones where that came from.

Like Tully Lake, its neighbor to the north, Little York is a glacial kettle hole with a deep central basin ringed by shallow, weedy bays and jutting peninsulas. The bays are havens for bass, pickerel and panfish; the basin is cold enough year-round to harbor trout.

Unlike many of the other small lakes in the region, Little York is readily accessible. It's paralleled on the east by I-81 and on the west by state Route 281. Dwyer Memorial Park, at the north end of the lake off Route 281, has ample parking and a very serviceable gravel boat-launch area. The main problem anglers face at Little York is competition with water skiers, whose hot-weather antics make the lake fishing an early-morning, late-evening affair when school's out.

If the skiers are hot-dogging too much, David merely paddles his canoe under I-81 and into Goodale Lake. Goodale, more of a pond than a lake, is less than five feet deep over most of its area. The notable exception is a seven-acre pothole at the north end. David happily works the shallow with his surface lures. Wedge, the trout fisherman, says anglers who come to Goodale in spring or fall sometimes pull a nice brown, or even a 12 to 14 inch brookie, from the deep end of the pond, which is fed by the cool current of the west branch of the Tioughnioga River.

Back in Little York, David haunts the lily pads along I-81 as well as the bays at the south end of the lake. Although he prefers the surface, some of his friends do quite well with spinner baits and plastic worms worked over, through and along the weed beds, David admitted.

Wedge likes to run glo-green Fireplugs, Sutton spoons and similar lures off his downrigger at depths of 20 to 50 feet, depending on the season and what his sonar equipment picks up. Generally, browns are found in shallower depths in spring and fall, and go deeper as the water warms. Any lure that approximates the resident yellow perch or alewives is apt to draw its share of strikes.

In the winter months, Little York's trout come within inches of the surface. It's one of the best places in the state to catch trout through the ice. Wedge says 10 pounders have been caught on minnows fished just two or three feet below the ice. Anglers on Little York can take up to 5 trout of any size per day.

The most common catches in winter, however, are pick-

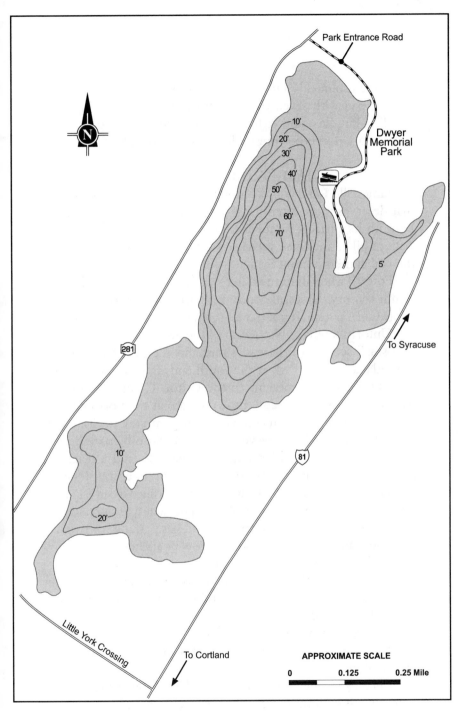

Figure 13.2   Little York Lake

erel, perch, bluegills and sunfish. Little York is a reliable place to fill a pail with seven to 10 inch perch on small shiners or Swedish Pimples, and it harbors some jumbo bluegills, too. Pickerel are numerous but seldom exceed 20 inches in length.

JAMESVILLE RESERVOIR

Jamesville Reservoir is an often overlooked body of water that deserves more attention from Central New York anglers. Beneath its surface, Jamesville hides a growing population of walleye pike, and state biologists rate the reservoir as one of the real comers among Syracuse area lakes.

Formed when Butternut Creek was dammed in the mid-nineteenth century, Jamesville once was an important feeder of the Barge Canal system. It now serves solely as a recreational resource.

Unfortunately, public access to the 333 acre lake is limited to a small section of the east shore and the Jamesville Beach Onondaga County Park at the south end. Even these vantage points pose some problems to the visitor. County Route 91 parallels the east shore and, near the dam at the north end of the reservoir, anglers can climb over the guard rail to cast lures or stillfish with bait. However, there's no close-by parking on the narrow road shoulder, and you'll have to find a place to pull off the highway north of the reservoir in order to fish here.

There is a private launch and boat livery called Toad's Landing on the West Shore Manor Road. The facility is open in the summer season from dawn to dusk and has parking for twenty cars and trailers. You may also rent row boats here.

In the county park there is no boat launch facility. However, fishermen with a small cartop rowboat or canoe can carry their craft and motor from the parking lot to the water, a distance of about 100 yards.

The extra effort could be rewarded with a mixed catch of walleyes, bass and panfish — or even a brown trout or tiger muskellunge.

Since 1983, the DEC has been stocking about 16,000 walleyed pike fingerlings per year in the reservoir, and gill netting revealed that several year classes of walleyes have prospered. The current limit is three with a minimum length of 18 inches.

The walleyes should make a big dent in the reservoir's massive schools of white perch, hopes Tom Chiotti, the aquatic biologist who monitors the reservoir for the DEC. Those perch are annoying pests to anyone who fishes Jamesville with a worm or other small bait. However, the perch and golden shiners are the main forage species in the lake, and will do their part to fatten up the walleyes.

Jamesville has thriving populations of smallmouth and large-mouth bass, too. Some of the bigmouths are whoppers. A few of five or six pounds are reported each season, although new-comers should more realistically hope for a stringer of one to two pounders.

Although walleyes and bass are Jamesville's bread and but-ter fish, the reservoir is capable of serving up a surprise or two for dessert. The DEC has made several plantings of 1,100-plus tiger muskies in recent seasons, and Chiotti expects the survi-vors to be pushing the 20 pound mark before long. The reser-voir also produces a nice brown trout now and then. The brown-ies swim downstream from Butternut Creek and stay to grow fat on the golden shiners and perch.

Jamesville Reservoir is also a melting pot of panfish species, with several different sunfish, rock bass, yellow perch and even a few pickerel. None of the panfish species seem to reach ex-ceptional size, but they do provide good fishing for shore an-glers in May and June.

The steep contours and bottom structure of the lake sug-gest a variety of tactics for those who want to focus on gamefish. The southern third of the reservoir is shallow and weedy, with a maximum depth of 15 feet. Here is the place to shop for a large-mouth bass, using surface baits or plastic worms. Chiotti said the DEC's nets also captured many walleyes in the weedbeds.

Walleyes also like to congregate at the edges of the steep drop-offs along the east shore. Smallmouths frequent the same area, along with the drop-offs in the northwest corner of the lake. Try a gold or silver finished Fat Rap or Rat-L-Trap plug to imitate the predominant forage fish.

For tiger muskies, anglers should concentrate on the weedbed edges early and late in the season. The tiger muskies in other lakes often suspend in deep water over drop-offs when the weather is hot, and there's no reason to think the Jamesville specimens will behave much differently.

Browns, while rare, are most often taken near the dam where the lake reaches its maximum depth of 36 feet.

Jamesville Reservoir has not been heavily utilized by ice fishermen, but if the walleye population continues to make gains, the lake has the potential to become one of the region's top spots for winter anglers.

DeRUYTER RESERVOIR

DeRuyter Reservoir is one of those productive little lakes that serious bass fishermen like to keep to themselves. The 560-acre reservoir has limited access and is subject to relatively light fishing pressure, despite excellent water quality and fish-holding structure.

Constructed in the 19th century as a water supply and feeder to the Erie Canal system, the reservoir is ringed by summer camps and year-round homes. Although it's only seven miles south of U.S. Route 20 and barely 30 miles as the crow flies from the state Thruway, the reservoir is tucked into the southwest corner of rural Madison County — apparently just far enough out of the way to deter most anglers from giving it a try.

Les Wedge, as senior aquatic biologist, electrofished DeRuyter for the DEC, says it's worthy of more attention than it gets.

"As a bass lake, I'd rate it equal to Tully Lake, although it's probably more difficult to fish," Wedge said.

Much of the difficulty lies in reading the lake. While Tully Lake has a mind boggling assortment of bays, drop-offs and weedbeds that are detectable at a glance, DeRuyter is more of a mystery. Viewed from the surface, it has just a handful of obvious fish magnets: a short point on the northwest shore, a large, foot-shaped peninsula jutting out from the west shore, and two small islands just north of the peninsula.

While these are all good places to fish, a tour of the lake with map in hand and the sonar turned on will reveal a few more prime spots, as well. The weedy southern third of the lake is a great location to snare bass on, for example, buzzbaits or weedless worm rigs, particularly early and late in the season.

DeRuyter is no deeper than 20 feet south of the peninsula, but plunges to a maximum of 55 feet at its north end before spilling out into the headwaters of Limestone Creek. The drop-off is precipitous here, and fishermen who don't pay close attention to their sonars may be casting into 30 or 40 feet of water when they thought they were working 10 to 20 foot depths.

This is a lake with some lunker largemouths. A six pounder would be considered unusual but not rare, says Wedge. Three pounders are common.

Although largemouths are the featured players at DeRuyter, walleye pike vie for top billing and take over the lead role in the winter months. Walleyes are caught regularly by deep trolling plugs such as numbers 7 and 9 perch-finish Rapalas or by drifting with Dixie Spinner and worm combinations along the east shore and around the peninsula. A few lunkers of six to eight pounds are taken each summer and again through the ice. Swedish Pimples or shiner minnows are the favored winter lures.

The reservoir also has fair numbers of smallmouth bass and fair to good fishing for pickerel. The pickerel will average 16 or 17 inches long.

Yellow perch, the main forage fish, along with golden shiners, provide good ice fishing opportunities, as do bluegills and crappies. DeRuyter also has some bullheads.

Access to the reservoir can be had at the Boathouse Restaurant, which maintains a small launch area at the south end. To reach it, take U.S. Route 20 to Cazenovia, then head south on state Route 13 for about 10 miles. When you come to Hunt Road (County Route 56), turn right. Take your second right onto East Lake Road, then go left on South Lake Road and look for the Boathouse on your right.

Chapter 14
THE FIVE BEST STREAMS
IN DEC REGION 8
by Len Lisenbee

That portion of New York included in DEC Region 8 is both unique and diversified with respect to its rivers and streams. There are two blue ribbon trout streams and numerous lesser known rivers and streams offering anglers a wealth of fishing opportunity, regardless of what species they might prefer to catch. Here is just a small sampling.

COHOCTON RIVER

The Cohocton River offers anglers a wide choice of trout fishing opportunity. From the native brook trout hiding in the narrow and shallow headwaters to trophy browns found throughout the more traditional-looking waters of the lower stretches, this river offers myriad challenges to the angler.

The headwaters of the river are in the Town of Springwater in Livingston County. In this hill country, it's easy to step across the "river" without getting your feet wet. This is native brook trout water. However, the stream is so overgrown in places that dapping with dry flies or drifting live bait are the only ways to fish most pools.

The middle stretch of the Cohocton extends from the Route 21 Bridge near Wayland to the first bridge on Route 415. This stretch is the most unlikely looking trout water a person ever set eyes on. The river flows through swampy wetlands for almost the entire distance. Long, slow pools of dark, often roily water appear to be more suitable for catfish than brown trout. But the appearance is misleading. There are some nice browns lurking in these cold, spring-fed waters.

Successfully fishing this stretch is no easy task. While there are some open areas where a flyrod can be used, much of this stream has a high canopy of overhanging vegetation that makes working a long rod almost impossible. A better choice would be ultralight spinning gear and tiny spinners and spoons or live bait such as worms or minnows.

This is ideal canoe water. The best way to fish this section is from one of these craft. Launch areas and some restricted parking is available at every bridge crossing the stream.

The lower reaches of the Cohocton River run from the first Route 415 bridge to its confluence with the Tioga River. For most of this distance, the Cohocton is a blue ribbon trout steam. Fast flowing riffles and rapids run into long deep pools. Route 415 parallels the river for most of the way.

There are two stretches of "trophy" water on the Cohocton. One runs from the northern boundary of the U.S. Veterans Hospital in Bath, N.Y. upstream to the first Route 415 bridge encountered. The second begins at the north boundary of the Village of Avoca and runs upstream to the mouth of Neils Creek. Both stretches are full of nice trout.

My favorite pool on this river actually lies just below the lower stretch of trophy waters. It stretches for over a hundred yards, passing under the entrance bridge to the VA Hospital. I don't know how many trout inhabit the depths here, but at noon on one bright sunny day I observed several hundred lying in the deepest part of the pool directly under the bridge. And on more than one occasion I have caught a trout on nearly every cast for an entire morning, moving less than twenty yards in the process.

Make no mistake, this is not always an easy stream to fish. There are educated trout, and making one rise often requires a perfect cast with a fly of the correct color and size. I also remember

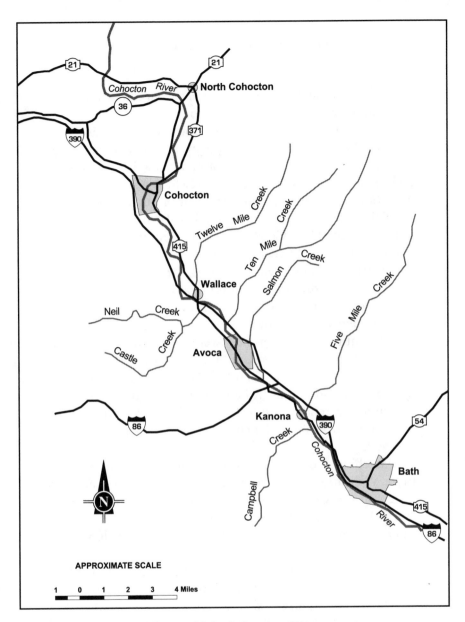

Figure 14.1   Cohocton River

days when you could only fish to a feeding trout and then you had to take it on the first cast or you lost your opportunity.

The Cohocton River is open for trout fishing all year. There are special regulations in the trophy waters. The limit is three trout per day and each trout must be at least 12 inches long. Only artificial lures can be used. Elsewhere anglers enjoy a 5 trout (any size) limit, and any legal bait or lure can be used.

This river has several tributaries that also hold nice populations of trout. Neils Creek is probably the best known, but don't overlook Goff Creek and Twelve Mile Creek. While Goff Creek is stocked annually with browns, there are some brookies lurking in its headwaters as well as in some of the deeper downstream pools. Trout carry-over is excellent, and a few browns manage to grow to trophy size.

The entire 20 miles of the lower Cohocton, from just below Atlanta to just downstream of Bath, appears to have been created with fly fishermen in mind. There is a natural progression of mayfly and caddisfly hatches. These begin shortly after ice-out and extend well into October. The size and duration of some of these insect hatches has to be experienced to be believed.

Matching the hatch, however, is important for success. Insect identification and realistic flies help, but the real key is matching the size and color of the naturals. Equally important is being able to present a size 20 or smaller dry fly or emerger without drag to rising trout on ultra-clear, slow-moving waters.

Anglers using spinning tackle with lures will find their best success comes with small silver or gold spinners. Old standbys like the Mepps Squirrel-Tail and Panther Martin spinners will produce some fish. Small gold or silver colored spoons also work well here.

Bait fishermen would be wise to stick with nightcrawlers, regardless of which stretch they might choose to fish. Other baits will work, but not with the regularity of fat, live nightcrawlers. Anglers using live bait should remember that bait possession is prohibited in the two "Trophy" stretches.

One possible exception to the "nightcrawler is the best bait" rule is a live grasshopper or cricket threaded on a thin wire hook and fished on two pound test line during late summer or early fall. I have not seen hotter fishing anywhere than on this river when I was gently roll-casting grasshoppers to hungry browns with a nine foot flyrod and a 7X tippet.

Angler access is good for most of the length of this river. Aside from Route 415 which parallels much of the lower stretches, there are lots of small country roads crossing the stream. Angler access sites with parking areas are provided near the trophy stretches. There is also parking available by permission on the VA Hospital grounds. Just check with security first.

CHEMUNG RIVER

The Chemung River, from its beginning at the confluence of the Tioga, Canisteo and Cohocton Rivers near Corning, downstream to its junction with the Susquehanna River near Waverly, is a highly productive warm water fishery. It is best known for its lunker walleyes, feisty smallmouth bass and a respectable population of panfish.

The physical characteristics of this river change with every bend. It ranges from swift narrow runs to wide shallow pools. The bottom continually changes from rocky pebbles to silt beds and shale rubble. There is a healthy but not overbearing growth of aquatic weeds. All of which encourages the wide variety of fish life found in these waters.

Most angling pressure on this river is directed at smallmouth bass. These gamefish can be found in good numbers in every fishable stretch. While the vast majority average between one and two pounds in weight, there are enough lunkers over four pounds lurking in the deeper holes to make fishing exciting.

One of the most famous stretches of smallmouth water is located above the Walnut Street Bridge near downtown Elmira. This is a stretch of runs and riffles that would be, were it only cooler, ideal trout water. Instead, this is classic smallmouth bass water.

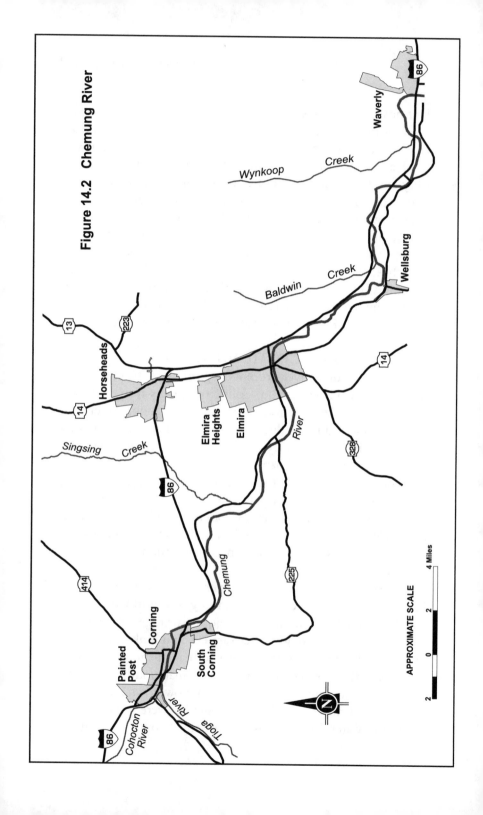

Figure 14.2 Chemung River

More good smallmouth water lies below the dam in Elmira, and another hotspot is the stretch around the mouth of Wyncoop Creek, especially anytime after a rain. It seems any increase in the inflowing water from that creek brings a smorgasbord of food for the hungry smallmouth in the area.

The walleye fishing in this river has been coming on strong during the past two decades. Good numbers can be found in any of the deeper holes. Probably the best walleye fishing is found below the dam in downtown Elmira (which also happens to be a hotspot for smallmouth bass).

If anglers were limited to only one lure on this river, it would have to be a number 5 or 7 sinking Rapala. This lure accounts for more bass and walleye than all other lures combined. It should be fished deep and slow for walleyes and slightly faster for bass.

Second place on the effective lure list goes to the ubiquitous jig. Light colors on light days and dark colors on dark days is the general rule. Tipping the hook with a piece of live worm, salted minnow or a Mister Twister plastic tail often adds just the right fish-catching touch to the lure's attractive properties.

The best live baits are minnows and worms. A nightcrawler rigged on a harness and drifted along the bottom of a deep run will account for more bass on the stringer, while live minnows will take more walleyes. Worms are especially effective for both species below the dam site mentioned earlier. They should be cast right to the base of the dam and allowed to roll downstream with the river flow.

Fisherman access to this river is good. Routes 352, 427 and I-86 parallel the river along much of its course. Parking is allowed along the first two. Most of the river can be waded, but caution is urged around swift runs and the deeper holes. There are numerous fishermen access points in Corning, Elmira and all the way to the Pennsylvania border for wading anglers.

Stretches of this river are often shallow and rocky, making it ideal for canoes and small boats. Both New York State and the Chemung County Federation of Sportsmen have developed several launch sites for cartoppers or very small trailered craft. These are located at Bottcher's Landing and Fitches Bridge on Route 352 and on Hendy Creek Road just off Route 427. Limited parking is available at each launch site.

MILL CREEK

Mill Creek is a pristine little stream flowing through Patchenville, Perkinsville and then down to Dansville. At Patchenville, it is only around 12 feet wide and a foot in depth, except in the occasional hole. But just below this village the creek gets a heavy inflow of cold spring water from the Wayland aquifer. It doubles its rate of flow within a mile.

The most intriguing fact about this stream is that it has more pounds of trout per acre than any other stream or river in New York, say Region 8 fisheries biologists. It isn't a stocked stream, either. Every one of the thousands of brown trout found here is a native.

Probably the best fishing is found in a mile long stretch running parallel to an old abandoned railroad bed. This bed can easily be located since it is an extension of the old Gunlock Factory line, and runs southeast from the railroad cars set up as a factory display along Route 21, just south of Wayland.

Flyrods should be left in the car. Because of the extensive overhanging brush, the only way to fish most of this creek is with an ultralight spinning rod and either live bait or tiny spinners. Anglers must use extra caution when they approach a pool. These native browns are extremely spooky and thus are also tough to catch.

Except for the railroad bed area and one other small stretch of public fishing access below Perkinsville, the stream flows entirely through private lands. Fishing is by landowner permission only. However, I have never been turned away by any landowners in the past.

Special fishing regulations cover Mill Creek. The limit is five trout, any size, per angler per day. Either bait or lures can be used. The stream is open for trout fishing all year.

OATKA CREEK

The headwaters of Oatka Creek flow out of Wyoming County. From there to just upstream of the Village of Mumford, this stream is a fair warm water fishery. It flows underground near Leroy and then re-emerges a few miles to the east with water only a few degrees cooler than where it sinks beneath the earth. Between the "Blue Hole," where the stream once again returns to the surface, and Mumford there are some bass and panfish. There is also the occasional trout. But for all intents and purposes, it is still a warm water fishery.

It isn't until after the cold, clear waters of Spring Creek flow into Oatka Creek at Mumford that this stream becomes cool enough to harbor trout. From the Village of Mumford, east to its junction with the Genesee River, this is a blue ribbon trout stream in every sense of the word.

Oatka Creek averages over fifty feet in width, and is near-classic pool and riffle trout water for its entire length. The pools are long and usually not too deep. The riffles are full of

Oatka Creek has all those ingredients that add up to classic fly fishing water.

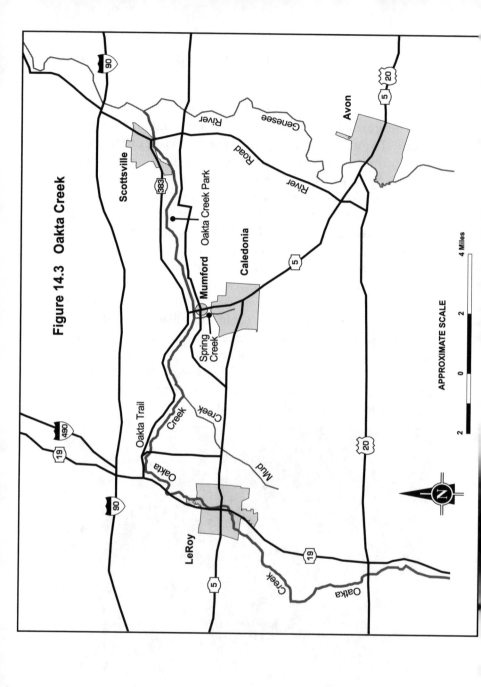

Figure 14.3 Oakta Creek

APPROXIMATE SCALE

4 Miles

productive pocket water. Most of the bottom is gravel, but there are some sandy stretches. There are also patches of weeds here and there, but most of the water runs free, clear and cold. This creek is truly a place where trophy trout dwell. The designated trophy water of just 1.7 miles is controversial with the local chapter of Trout Unlimited, so check your Fishing Regulations Guide for the exact location. But an angler offering the right fly pattern or lure anywhere on this stream or on Spring Creek might just raise a three-pound plus brown trout.

Don't expect to find any easy-to-catch or stocked trout in these waters. The only stocked fish found here are the occasional escapees from the DEC hatchery in Caledonia, two miles south of Mumford. Wild brown trout are the predominant inhabitants of these waters, which means anglers have to be at the top of their game if they expect to catch any Oatka or Spring Creek trout.

This stream offers excellent mayfly hatches. Most of the classic ones are here: little blue dun in early April; the quill gordon in mid to late April; pale evening dun and March brown in early and late May and early June; light cahill and gray fox from late May through June; and tiny olive duns and diminutive *Tricorythodes*, *Caenis* and *Baetis* throughout the late summer and into the fall months.

Late in the season it isn't unusual for anglers to use 7X or even 8X tippets and size 20 to 24 flies. The low, clear waters encountered here after mid-July often dictate the use of these tiny flies. This challenge is magnified when the target fish is one of the larger browns.

In addition to the mayflies, fly fishermen will also find a wide selection of (mostly) green, dark gray and dark brown caddis flies. There are even several remarkable stonefly hatches, but no one has been able to correctly predict their emergence from year to year. Look for them anytime from mid-June to mid-August.

The Caledonia Fish Hatchery, by the way, is the cradle of modern fish culture in the United States. Seth Green realized

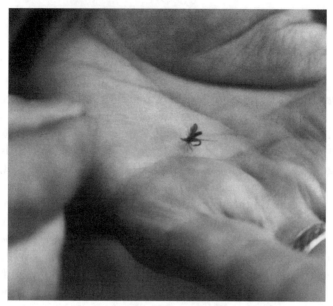

On Oatka Creek, small flies such as this #20 olive are the rule more often than the exception.

that as a hatchery site, this place was a natural. The cold, crystal-clear artesian waters of Spring Creek boil out of the ground in Caledonia, less than a mile above the hatchery.

Regulations for Oatka Creek outside the trophy section are the same as New York's general trout regulations: five trout of any size per angler per day with live bait or lures being legal. In the trophy water it is no kill and only artificial lures are allowed. Fishing is permitted all year in both sections.

Fishing regulations below the well marked special regulations sections at the hatchery are different still. Anglers can fish all year for trout, and no more than five trout per day can be kept. Fish must be at least nine inches long, and any bait or lure is allowed.

There is a short stretch of special regulations water just below the hatchery reserved for handicapped anglers. This stretch is easily fished from shore. It is also wheel-chair accessible, which brings the possibility of quality fishing and trophy trout to handicapped anglers otherwise excluded from this fine sport.

There is another short stretch of water above the hatchery open to fly fishing only. No wading is allowed, your limit is three trout and they must be 10 inches or longer. Still, this stretch is a must for any died-in-the-wool trout angler. The numerous trout swimming just a few feet away in ultra-clear water are enough to start the adrenaline flowing in the veins of even the most experienced fly fisherman.

There is adequate angler parking available along Spring and Oatka Creeks. Anglers wanting to fish Spring Creek are welcome to park at the hatchery, and there is space available next to the old railroad depot, located just north (downstream) of the hatchery. Use caution when walking along the railroad tracks to the stream. This is an active rail line. There is also parking in the lot of the Second Baptist Church in Mumford for anglers wishing to sample the lower stretches of this creek.

Both the DEC and the local chapter of Trout Unlimited maintain numerous angler parking areas along Oatka Creek. There's canoe access from the lot at the intersection of Routes 36 and 383. (Canoes are fun, but not needed here). Route 383 generally parallels this creek all the way to Scottsville, with several angler pull-offs located on the south side of the road along the way.

Additional creek access points are located on every road crossing the creek. One of the best starting points is the parking lot behind the country store on Bowerman Road. Another is located where Armstrong Road crosses the creek, just downstream from Mumford. Anglers should not have trouble finding a parking space. The biggest decision is where to start fishing on this stream.

GENESEE RIVER

The Genesee River from Mount Morris to Rochester is a warm water fishery. It is best known for good to excellent walleye fishing and fair to good smallmouth bass fishing. In fact, some locals claim that a well presented nightcrawler, minnow or jig will catch a nice walleye anytime, day or night. Many bass are caught incidental to walleye fishing.

There is also some excellent northern pike fishing around the mouths of tributaries and along the wider weed bed areas just south of Rochester. The mouth of Oatka Creek, with its extensive weed beds and relatively shallow waters, is probably the best known pike water. The mouth of Black Creek and the area around the Barge Canal are also proven producers of big northerns, including some exceeding 20 pounds.

One problem often encountered here is roily water conditions. In fact, with agriculture and dam outflows occuring along much of this river, the best water condition that can be hoped for seems to be slightly murky. But it doesn't seem to adversely affect the walleye fishing.

Angler access on this river is limited. There are a number of bridges crossing between Mt. Morris and Rochester, but banks are steep and safe off-road parking is limited. One good boat launching point is located on North Road just east of Scottsville and Route 383. Canoes and cartop rigs can be launched here. Small motors are extremely useful in getting to the better fishing holes more quickly.

Chapter 15
THE FIVE BEST PONDS/LAKES IN DEC REGION 8
by Len Lisenbee

C entral New York is best known to anglers for its Finger Lakes, a series of glacial lakes with deep, cold, productive waters. Few people realize that this portion of the Empire State is also blessed with small lakes and numerous ponds that are equally bountiful fish producers.

LAMOKA LAKE

Lamoka Lake is located south of Route 23 in the Town of Tyrone. It contains one of the most notable warm water fisheries in the region. It is 43 feet at its deepest point, with a mean depth of around 20 feet. The surface area is 588 acres. There are extensive yet fishable weed beds everywhere.

The weed beds are a significant part of this lake's excellent productivity. They provide shelter for a dense forage base and small gamefish. In addition, there is an established population of sawbellies that assist in feeding twelve species of game and panfish. Most anglers spend their time searching for bass — mostly largemouth, but there is a small resident population of smallmouth, too. A lot of five pound plus largemouths are caught here each year, and recent DEC samplings revealed several bass in the eight to ten pound range.

Lamoka Lake smallmouths rarely exceed three pounds. Their habitat isn't nearly as widespread or productive as the lake's bigmouth habitat. There are plenty of sculpins and cray-fish in the forage base, but other requirements for this species, such as cooler, less weedy waters, are not really met. Nonethe-less, anglers using live bait, light colored jigs or other ploys sometimes collect stringers of scrappy bronzebacks.

The best lures for Lamoka Lake largemouth bass include Rapalas and Rebels, as well as plastic worms (purple and black) and soft-bodied spinnerbaits. Live bait such as sawbellies, cray-fish (locally known as "crabs") and nightcrawlers work well here, and account for many of the bass taken each year. Night fishing with surface lures such as the Jitterbug or Lucky-13 bring some spectacular results. Ask local anglers like Gary Edmister, Jr. who can tell you that night is when the big ones come out to feed. He is still talking about the one that got away, a bass that had a mouth like a tunnel and was at least twenty inches long in the light of the moon.

While bass are the most commonly targeted species, this lake has a lot more to offer anglers. The chain pickerel popula-tion is very high, and there are some five-pound plus pickerel caught every year. The preferred method is drifting with live minnows. Minnow-imitating lures and noisy surface lures also work well at times.

Panfish angling here can be exceptional. Yellow perch and crappie are the most sought after. Many one-pound plus fish are taken on live minnows suspended from a bobber or just above a light sinker. Slab-sided members of the bluegill family weighing nearly a pound are also common. They are taken on just about everything from flyrod poppers and small surface plugs to nightcrawlers fished slowly along the bottom.

The glamour fish of Lamoka Lake is the muskellunge. This species is listed as "uncommon" by the DEC, and few people actually fish solely for them here. New York doesn't stock muskies in this lake any more. Still, every year at least a dozen trophies are brought to net, with some of them tipping the scales at over 25 pounds. Most successful anglers stick with traditional musky lures trolled fast along weedlines, or large,

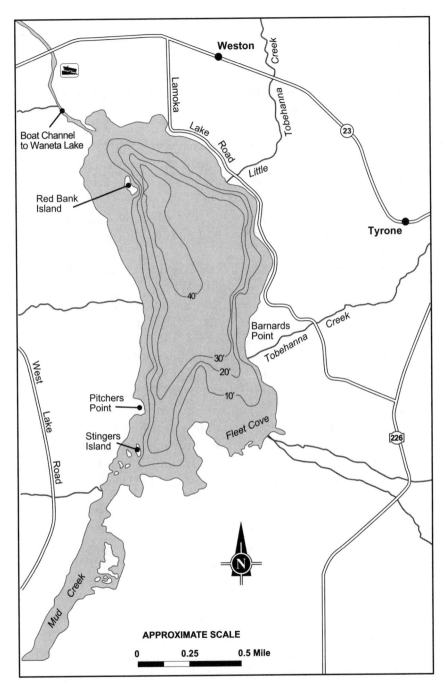

Figure 15.1 Lamoka Lake

live minnows suspended from a bobber in a weedbed opening or along a weedline.

Fishing is not always easy; there are extensive weedbeds everywhere. While the lake is not what you would call choked out, being able to successfully fish weedy areas is critical to success. This means knowing how various lures react in order to keep them just over or just out of the weeds. Time tested weedless lures like the Johnson Silver Minnow annually account for a major share of bass and pickerel, along with a few muskies.

DEC, in conjunction with New York Electric and Gas, has established a boat launch site on the Waneta-Lamoka Channel next to the Route 23 bridge. There are actually two grooved concrete ramps separated by Route 23, allowing anglers access to either of these fine lakes. However, it will probably be necessary to pull a boat and then re-launch it on the other ramp if both lakes are to be fished. The reason is the relatively small round culvert pipe (approximately eight feet wide and with only about four feet of clearance in the center) connecting the two lakes. Canoes and boats with less than four feet of beam and a low profile shouldn't have any problems passing through. All vehicle and trailer parking is on the south side of Route 23.

Don't use the channels just as access to the lakes. They too hold plenty of fish, especially bass and panfish.

WANETA LAKE

Waneta Lake, at over 800 acres, has a larger surface area than Lamoka. It is also shallower and even weedier, with a maximum depth of 30 feet and a mean depth of 15 feet. The bottom is a patchwork of gravel-sand and muck-sediment.

The shoreline is more regular than Lamoka Lake, roughly forming a long narrow rectangle running almost due north and south. There are extensive wetlands around much of its southern shoreline. Route 25 parallels the east shore while the Waneta Lake Road parallels the west shore. The Village of Wayne is just north of the lake.

This lake, like its sister to the south, has a healthy forage base for predatory gamefish. And like Lamoka Lake, an impressive roster of catchable fish species call Waneta Lake home. These include both largemouth and smallmouth bass, muskellunge, chain pickerel, yellow perch, black crappies, and several species of panfish.

Most anglers spend their time chasing the ample population of bass. Largemouth have been found by DEC electro-shock survey crews at just under 10 pounds. One of the best locations for these fish is in the channel leading to the lake from the boat launch ramp. It takes some special care to fish this water because your boat will normally announce your approach. But by using an electric motor and then waiting for silence to return to the water, you have a chance to connect with some trophy sized bass. There is also a lot of ideal habitat in the southeast corner of the lake where timber was flooded over to make this impoundment that serves as a reservoir to the hydro-electric plant on Keuka Lake.

The smallmouth bass of Waneta must contend with several factors that adversely affect them. Because of the extensive weeds, they are basically restricted to the small area in this lake with good gravel bottom along the east side. Since that is only around one-tenth of the overall lake bottom area, it is obvious these fish are not nearly as common as largemouths. It is also why the smallmouth are smaller, averaging just over a pound in weight and rarely exceeding two.

Both species of bass will fall for live minnows. Suspend them three to ten feet below a bobber. Or add some split shot a foot or so up the line and allow them to bump bottom during a drift of weedless areas. Nightcrawlers and crabs can be substituted, usually with equally pleasing results.

Most anglers, however, spend at least a portion of their time throwing artificial lures at these fish. Most popular are Rapalas and similar floating minnow imitations. Hot-n-Tots and spinnerbaits are also popular, especially early in the season. Proficient plastic worm anglers will have good results from swimming purple, black or natural colored worms rigged Texas style (weedless) and fished just over the tops of weed beds or crawled slowly across the bottom.

Night fishing for bass is popular. Loud, splashy, surface lures like the Jitterbug and Chugger, worked slowly through openings in the weeds, have accounted for some fine catches of largemouths. When the fish ignore these and similar offerings, local anglers often switch to floating Rapalas and twitch them softly across the surface.

Without doubt, the muskellunge is the glamour fish of this lake. The musky population here is both larger and more stable than that of Lamoka. DEC stocks almost 5,000 muskies per year, a sizeable number for such a small lake. DEC biologist David Kosowski has speculated that this body of water could potentially produce the next state record, upsetting the long standing title held by the St. Lawrence River at 69 pounds, 15 ounces set in 1957 by Arthur Lawton.

In a recent DEC netting survey of the lake, a 52 inch-trophy estimated to weigh in excess of 50 pounds was found. The fish was later aged by a scale sample to be in the range of 20 years old said Senior Fisheries Biologist Kosowski. The fish was carefully released back into Waneta after the measurements were taken. In addition to the giant female, the same survey turned up trophy muskies of 45, 44, and 42 inches.

Annual DEC stockings ensure the future for this species. Growth rates are excellent, and every year there are a number of 25 pound plus fish caught. The late Fred Tanner caught three muskies over 30 pounds in the fall of 1986. He trolled Pikie Minnows along the weedlines. The unofficial hook and line record is 38 pounds. Most muskies are caught during October and November.

Catching these giant fish is not too difficult. Most anglers use either the large traditional plugs such as the Creek Chub series or large Rebel or Rapala jointed-minnow imitations. These are trolled rapidly along the edge of weedbeds. It is often necessary to add two to four ounces of lead, either in-line or as a drop sinker, in order to reach the range of 15 to 20 feet below

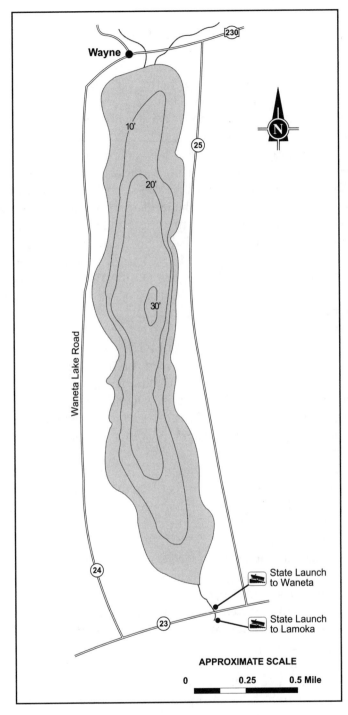

Figure 15.2   Waneta Lake

the surface on a fast troll. Or better yet, use downriggers to control trolling depths. Wire leaders are a necessity anytime muskies are the target species. Most will use a 12-inch steel leader rated at 30 pound-test.

There always seems to be at least one species of panfish actively hitting lures or baits. Usually it's the crappie or yellow perch grabbing the headlines, but big, slab-sided bluegills and overgrown rock bass also put on the feedbag with quiet regularity.

Anglers should take note that the .7 mile channel connecting these two lakes has yielded eight pound plus bass, more than a few large muskies and is a known producer of good stringers of crappie and bluegills. During the first few weeks after ice out, anglers may also fill a pail or two with tasty brown bullheads.

CAYUTA LAKE

Just east of Route 228, between Alpine and Mecklenburg in the Town of Catharine, lies diminutive Cayuta Lake. This quiet little lake rarely if ever has its waters crowded with either boaters or anglers. Yet its 371 acres harbors some lunker largemouth bass and chain pickerel, as well as six other gamefish species.

This lake is shallow, having a mean depth of only 14 feet and a maximum depth of 26 feet. There's no rule as to what particular part of the lake might be hot for any given fish species. Anglers are just as likely to catch a bass or pickerel with any cast of a lure.

Other game and panfish species include bullhead, rock bass, pumpkinseed, bluegills and yellow perch. Walleye used to be found here in abundance, but the increased aquatic plant growth has apparently reduced their numbers to just a few old and very big lunkers. Most walleye are now caught incidental to other species.

Ice fishing is quite popular here, with every species except bullhead a target. While most anglers try for the ample supply of yellow perch, a few lucky fishermen manage to bring up lunker largemouth bass in excess of five pounds. These are great fun but out of season and must be returned immediately. Chain pickerel approaching four pounds are also fairly common late in the ice fishing season.

Warm weather anglers used to be closed out of this lake by early July. Weed growth was horrible. However, the DEC started a weed removal program in 1988, and weed cutters now open enough water to keep bass anglers happy. Because of the weed control activity, bass and pickerel anglers can experience good catches through the entire season.

There is a serious lack of public access on this lake. The DEC has an open gravel launch site at the north end, but the water is so shallow that only cartop boats, canoes and very light trailer boats can be launched there. Parking is available at this site for several dozen vehicles, with or without trailers. There is no fee.

There is additional access to the lake on the south end at Cayuta Lake Camp. These folks have a gravel boat ramp on the lake outlet. It's a short run to the lake proper from there. This establishment sells bait and tackle, and rents boats by the day and cabins or campsites for the night or week. The boat launch fee is $5.

Cool-Lea Campgrounds off Route 228 along the western shore is a seasonal campground that also offers a gravel boat launch ramp, a bait shop and camping sites for rent. There is also a small lunchroom and cold drinks available at the camp. The launch fee is $5.

The Cayuta Lake outlet should not be overlooked by anglers. For the first mile or so after leaving the lake, it is an average warm water fishery. But after the first mile, this stream picks up a healthy shot of cold spring water. It then becomes superb trout habitat. It remains trout water all the way to its junction with the Susquehanna River near Waverly, PA.

Much of the access to this creek is across private lands. But area landowners are generally not too protective about their riparian rights. Access is quite often given with any friendly request.

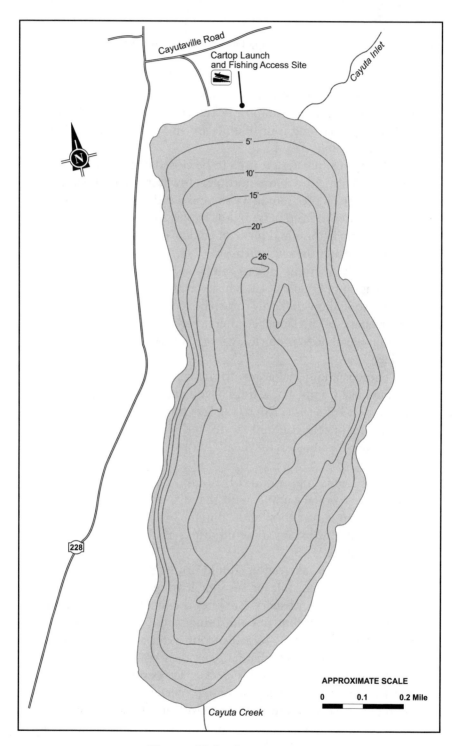

Figure 15.3 Cayuta Lake

New York has purchased several miles of permanent fishing access rights along this trout stream. Since these areas are broken up, anglers are advised to look for the yellow Public Fishing Area posters located along the shoreline. Parking is available in the two established parking areas and all along Routes 224 and 34. Both roads parallel this creek.

The stream is open to year-around fishing. There is some natural brook and brown trout reproduction, but most of the fish found here are stocked trout. While they might be somewhat easier to catch than their wild cousins, these fish are anything but pushovers. It takes a well-presented fly, lure or natural bait to fool them consistently.

FINGER LAKES NATIONAL FOREST PONDS

There are over two dozen fishable ponds located deep in the heart of the Finger Lakes National Forest. Most of these hold fair to good populations of gamefish. It is here that anglers can sample semi-backcountry seclusion as they try to catch either warm water bass and panfish or frisky trout.

During the last century this area was farmland, much of it awarded to veterans. The land was marginal at best for farming, and the owners abandoned the property one after another. The federal government started buying back the farms in 1934. There are now 16,000 plus acres of patchwork public lands. Approximately one-third is currently managed for livestock grazing while the remaining two-thirds is managed for multiple use.

Most of the ponds average less than half an acre, but every pond contains some catchable fish. Usually these will be various members of the sunfish family or brown bullheads, but there could be some nice largemouth bass lurking in any one of them. All of these species were stocked in every pond at one time or another.

Three ponds on the Forest Reserve hold trout. Foster, Potomac and Ballard Ponds receive annual stocking of both brook and rainbow trout courtesy of the United States Forest

Service, and fishing is on a put and take basis. These ponds are relatively shallow and tend to heat up during the summer months. The warm water means trout holdover is improbable.

Foster Pond also gets an annual stocking, which might include brookies, rainbows or browns. However, this pond is deeper and receives an influx of cold spring water at several points. Because of these conditions, trout holdover for a year or more has been documented.

Most anglers fishing any of these ponds usually stick with garden hackle (worms) or live minnows. But any well-presented lure including flies or poppers can also produce some fish. Fly casting can be a problem on a few ponds because of overgrown shorelines. Spin fishermen using bobbers to cast their flies often have the best of both worlds.

Getting to this unique area is part of the fun. It is located between Seneca and Cayuga Lakes and shares the border between Schuyler and Seneca Counties. It is in the towns of Hector, Covert and Lodi. The village of Watkins Glen is approximately 14 miles to the southwest, while the city of Ithaca is 16 miles east. Route 414 runs north and south along the western edge of Seneca and Schuyler Counties, and just to the west of this area.

County Route 2 south of Hector on Route 414 will take anglers past the Blueberry Patch Recreation Site and into the middle of the forest. Most of the ponds are off the Potomac Road, the main north and south road through the forest. Camping sites are available at Blueberry Patch for $5 per night, but free camping is available throughout the unimproved forest lands.

A good idea for first-time visitors is to stop at the ranger station on Route 414 near Hector and pick up a free map-brochure of the forest. You may also purchase a special topographic map, made from parts of 6 quadrangles, for $3.00. These nicely detailed maps not only locate every small pond,

John Fisher bringing home dinner in the form of some tasty brook trout, taken from Foster Pond, Finger Lakes National Forest.

they also delineate parking areas and hiking trails. Included in the brochure is a short list of area rules and safety tips worth noting.

HIGH TOR WILDLIFE MANAGEMENT AREA PONDS

The High Tor (sometimes spelled Hi Tor) Wildlife Management Area stretches from the extensive wetlands at the south end of Canandaigua Lake to the hilltops on the eastern side of that lake. Approximately 6,000 acres of wilderness-like lands fall within the boundaries of this unique area, and there is some good pond fishing available.

There are eight fishable ponds located within the boundaries of High Tor in addition to the West River, a tributary to Canandaigua Lake. But severe winter ice conditions periodically kill all the fish in seven of those ponds, including the brook trout once found in the beaver flow at the head of Flint Creek. Only the bass and panfish found in the deepest and largest pond near the main service road survive year in and year out. The DEC restocks all of the waters as needed.

Getting to the ponds is not difficult, but does entail driving some rough country roads. From the Village of Naples, take East Hill Road to the intersection with Bassett Road. The management area entrance is just a short distance up Bassett Road. Parking is available in the DEC maintained and well-marked parking area. The ponds are located off the unnamed service roads.

High Tor Wildlife Management Area is a beautiful and unique wilderness-like area located in southwestern Yates County. To get there, drive to Naples at the south end of Canandaigua Lake. Then travel 2.2 miles north on Route 245. There is both an east and west entrance with appropriate DEC signs posted along Route 245. Free maps containing clear directions to this area are available from the DEC Region 8 office in Avon, NY, and are a handy item to have when traveling through this rural area.

These are just a small sampling of the outstanding angling opportunities available in this region of New York. There are

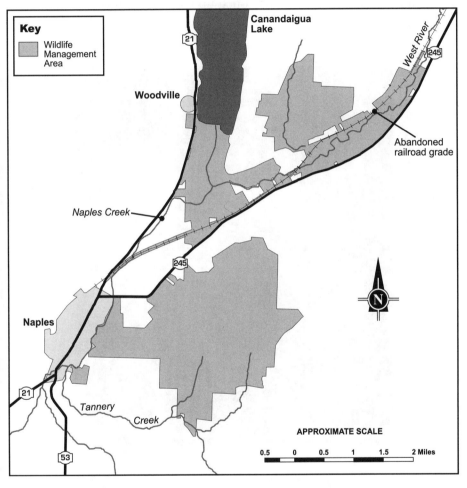

Key

Wildlife Management Area

Canandaigua Lake

West River

Woodville

Abandoned railroad grade

Naples Creek

Naples

Tannery Creek

APPROXIMATE SCALE

0.5   0   0.5   1   1.5   2 Miles

Figure 15.4   High Tor Wildlife Management Area

other wildlife management areas and state forest lands offering both stocked and natural trout and bass fishing, and literally thousands of private farm ponds and small lakes. A polite request of the landowner will open up most of them to you.

Chapter 16
THE FIVE BEST STREAMS IN DEC REGION 9
by David L. Barus

Western New York inland streams are one of our best kept fishing secrets!

For the record, inland streams are considered those streams which are not a direct tributary to one of the Great Lakes. Or, if a dam or natural waterfall exists on a tributary of the Great Lakes that is impassible by fish, the waters above the barrier are considered "inland stream waters." The success enjoyed in the Great Lakes has enhanced the inland fisheries. It has relieved the once intense fishing pressure found on the better Western New York inland streams.

Wiscoy Creek, East Koy Creek, Ischua Creek, the Genesee River upstream from Belmont and the upper portion of Cattaraugus Creek are all quality waters. While these streams are generally regarded as trout habitat, other species are also encountered.

WISCOY CREEK

Managed as a "wild trout" fishery, Wiscoy is one of the premier trout streams in the region and perhaps the state. Many say its angling opportunity is unequalled in the spring to autumn months.

Al Himmel, avid dry fly angler, Western New York Trout Unlimited member and a colorful character who inspires

An electrofishing survey being conducted on Wiscoy Creek, one of the blue ribbon trout streams of Western New York. (Courtesy DEC)

enthusiasm for fishing, related a recent experience he had while assisting the DEC during electro-shocking efforts.

"It's hard for a sane angler to believe how many fish are in the Wiscoy, and really good size fish too," said Himmel. "Many run 16 to 19 inches in length, all native trout."

There are lots of big trout, but they're not in the open as you may already have guessed, Himmel said. The older fish are under trees, bushes, overhanging banks, and in other hard to get to places.

"These native fish are very colorful and full of jump and splash when fooled on a fly," Himmel said. "The smaller fish are near the weirs, wing dams and obvious stream structure. Either way, it's an experience that is hard to match."

Himmel's reflections say it all. Recent stream sampling by DEC biologists revealed an adult wild brown trout population of over 1,500 fish per mile.

Wiscoy Creek meanders through the grazing pastures and farmlands of Eagle and Pike townships in Wyoming County. It eventually reaches Allegany County and descends through a cascading series of waterfalls at Mills Mills, before eventually reaching the Genesee River. The area between Pike and Mills

Mills, off Camp Road, is rated as the best trout water.

Largely spring fed, the Wiscoy is able to maintain cool-water ambience all summer long. Summer will find water levels low, but not nearly as low, or as warm, as most other inland streams.

Abundant insect hatches can occur on the stream throughout the year, accounting for the excellent growth rate and angling potential. The stream is open to anglers using spinners, small jigs and even tiny plugs, but the pristine nature of the stream seems to cultivate fly fishermen, especially during the summer months. Live bait is prohibited on certain sections of the stream reserved for artificials only.

Ultralight spinners will catch fish during the early trout season months of April and May. They will work during summer, but only when rising waters occur after a thunderstorm. Of course, spinners can catch a lot of trees too! I have been known to take a limit of willows on more than one occasion from the tiny casting lanes of certain upper Wiscoy areas. The $\frac{1}{18}$ ounce (#00) and $\frac{1}{12}$ ounce (#0) ultralight Mepps are good spinner selections, though miniature Panther Martin and C.P. Swings are also effective. The #00 Mepps pattern with a small, single hook Wooly-Bugger trailer is a real killer on the Wiscoy. Work the spinner by casting upstream through a riffle or adjacent to a hole. Retrieve down-current just a little faster than the rate of flow. As stream width and overhanging trees permit, angle casts slightly across current to cover the stream section completely.

Flies will catch a lot of fish in April too. Dave Tooke, a Lewiston resident and past president of Western New York Trout Unlimited, uses nymphs and wet flies in the early season. Tooke says, "While #14 and #16 Hendricksons are the fly of protocol in early April and May, sometimes the trout feel like a mouthful, and then #6 or #8 stonefly nymphs are really productive. When the stream is a little roily or muddy, streamers like the Mickey Finn and Muddler Minnow are excellent variations to normal early season wet flies." Tooke ties his streamer patterns on #9672 Mustad hooks and presents them on a 7½ foot, 4X leader.

In May, the more traditional dry fly fishing begins.

"Fishing during a hatch is great fun," said the late Rick Kinecki, of the Williamsville Orvis Shop. Kinecki suggested, "Mid-May patterns like the #14 Hendrickson and #16 to #18 Blue Dun are effective. By late May the #16 Grey Fox is also a good pattern."

During the height of summer, dry flies will produce best. Careful presentation of the right pattern is also necessary. To be successful you must learn to match the hatch, and a high degree of casting skill will also be needed. But there are many sections of the stream that will allow easy fly casting and still yield good fishing results. The Pike dam and town park is one place where you can observe large trout swimming in the pool below during warm summer days. These fish don't seem to bite on much of anything. Their size, however, is testament that they must eat sometime, probably at night.

A major trib of Wiscoy Creek is Trout Brook. The junction of these two creeks occurs just upstream from the Albro Road bridge, about two miles west of Pike on Route 39.

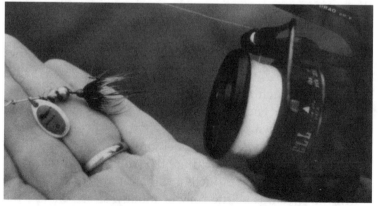

Small bucktailed spinners are often deadly medicine for early season trout in the small streams of New York's western tier.

Trout Brook supports a quality of angling similar to that found on the Wiscoy. Not a big stream, it is only 15 to 20 feet wide on average. Trout Brook falls into a special class. My late friend Cliff Train used to say, "It's a raaainn crik." When Cliff said that, he always made you grin. He meant it usually remained clear when other streams in the area were muddy with runoff. The dense brush along each bank helps to retain the wild and clear nature of this little "crik."

When I was a young boy, my father often brought the family here to enjoy early season trout fishing, and I'm still thanking him! The area is fishy looking and days on this stream are simply precious. While it is difficult to cast to its narrow winding runs, it is a stream where an angler can truly enjoy "private water" on a public fishing stream. Wild brook trout live here too. Between them and the wild brown trout, Trout Brook is appropriately named and doubly special.

The quality of the Wiscoy has been enhanced by the volunteer efforts of conservationists. Wing dams, cribbing, willow tree planting and other stream improvements are evidence of the commitment of dedicated anglers of Trout Unlimited and others.

Soft-spoken dry-fly expert Jim Keech comments on the Trout Brook/Wiscoy junction, "It's not an easy section to fish and the selective nature of the trout can be infuriating during summer months."

There are some good size fish, to 18 inches, that seem to live underneath the well-formed cribs, he said. The pool at Trout Brook, in particular, seems to be filled with rising browns that ignore any angler offering less than fly speck size, he noted.

"When no flies are hatching, float an attractor fly, a #14 or #16 hair wing Royal Coachman or Goofus Bug, alongside the cribbing," advises Keech. "In presenting the dry fly, float the fly as close as possible to the cribbings and wing dams, no more than six inches away."

The open pools of the Wiscoy are also productive, but also more unpredictable. Working the rises may require long leaders, to 14 and 18 feet, with 6X and 7X tippets.

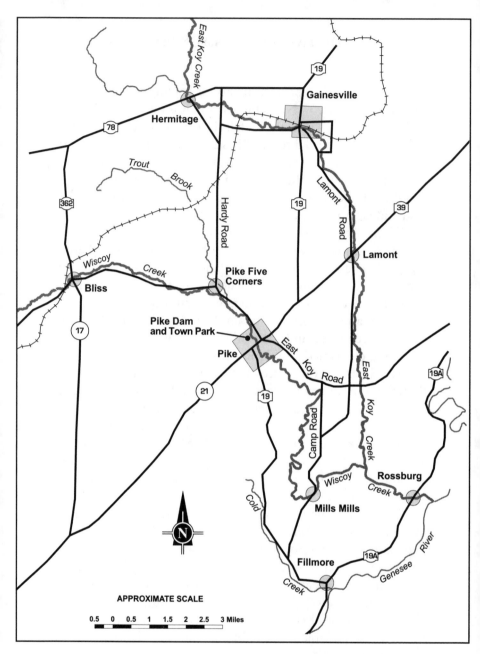

Figure 16.1 Wiscoy Creek and East Koy Creek

While an attractor fly will produce occasional fish in the pools, matching the hatch exactly is much more productive. From mid-June on, try a #14 Light Cahill to match the usually good evening hatches. As the summer advances, typical trout stream tactics apply and fly presentations need to get smaller. Try #18 thorax duns, #18 to #22 cream variants, #18 and #20 Fluttering Grey and Brown Caddis. In August, #22 black ants fished up against overhanging willows are good. In September, go back to bigger flies.

There are more than 12 miles of Public Fishing Rights in the Wyoming County section of Wiscoy Creek and numerous public parking and access points located all along the stream. All are clearly marked. Because of the abundance of wild trout in the Wyoming County portion, no stocking is necessary. In the lower portion of the stream in Allegany County, from Mills Mills upstream to the county line, a 1.2-mile section is stocked annually with 750 brown trout.

Wiscog Creek has a 10 inch size limit and three trout per day creel limit. A special catch-and-release and artificial lures only area spans the water a half-mile on either side of the East Hillside Road bridge.

EAST KOY CREEK

The East Koy is another one of the many diverse inland streams in Western New York. It's located principally in Wyoming County.

The East Koy is stocked from the Allegany County line upstream to Hermitage, approximately 13 miles, with over 11,000 brown trout per year. Within this distance are some 11.9 miles of easements allowing Public Fishing Rights. Several tributaries of the East Koy have wild brown trout and native brook trout, including the headwaters of the stream above Hermitage, near Wethersfield Springs.

These upper reaches are typical of Wyoming County headwaters, and are characterized by dense overgrowth. Ultralight spinning with tiny spinners like #00, #0 and #1 sizes is effective, and early season fishing with worms or salted minnows can also be good.

From Hermitage to Gainesville, the original fast running water transforms into a slower, wider stream. There are good pools in this section, but many exist near open pasture land, making an undetected approach more difficult. The deep pools at the Hermitage bridge offer potential for large carry-over trout. As Al Himmel and Jim Keech forecast, the worm fisherman should have good results here. After leaving Hermitage, the creek passes through a dense swamp and woodlands, almost impossible to reach except by following the B&O railroad tracks off Shearing Road. There are definitely some large fish in this section too.

Once through the lowland swamp, the creek meanders alongside Shearing Road. There is easy access here, and heavy stocking at the end of March and again at the onset of May. This makes for good family outings with generally easy catches of hatchery trout. There is also a campground here, and all of the nearby creek waters are open to the public. This is a good area with a few deep pools, a few riffles and a few cribbings. Early in the year using ultralight spinning tackle, I have been fortunate to fool both wild brown and native brook trout on the same trip.

The creek crosses Route 19 at Gainesville, where water volume and flow rate pick up. The creek follows Lamont Road to the intersection of School House Road, where a bridge provides good access. There is a huge, deep pool below the bridge that offers excellent bait fishing from shore. The fish here are generally stockers, but one or two big natives are also taken every year.

The stream above the pool is filled with riffles, small pools and good in-water structure. It is excellent early season spinner water, and will entertain May and June fly fishermen as well.

At the Metcalf Road bridge, the pool below holds good numbers of fish. From the bridge upstream, there are also a number of good pools, excellent riffles and areas of overhanging willows that hold big trout. There is fallen timber and several good "turns" in the creek before it gets to Jordan Road. Spin fishing anglers share success here in the early season until June, when fly anglers take over.

The Jordan Road bridge pool is heavily stocked, and thus a good area to take the kids on that first trip of the year. There is access at the bridge, and parking nearby. A campsite is located near the bridge. This whole section offers good green drake hatches, and the March brown is in abundance too.

Upstream from the Murphy Road bridge is classic rocky bottom riffle fishing. The fish will inhale a nymph or wet fly fished deep or along the bank of the pools found here. Al Himmel favors a Calftail-Hairwing Coachman tied Wulff style during summer months. The entire section, from Murphy Road to Metcalf Road, can be fished in about four hours, ideal for an evening outing.

From Murphy Road to Lamont, the one mile stretch of stream is best described as "ideal." There are numerous pools and riffles.

A summary of patterns for the middle East Koy include: Blue Quill (#18) in April, Hendrickson (#14) in May, Light Cahills (#14) in June, and Trico (#18, #20, #22 & #24) in July and August and even into September. The Trico hatches occur between 1 p.m. and 9 p.m. and later as the season progresses. The local experts may also use a #18 Tan Caddis into late August.

From Lamont Road to East Koy Road, posted signs interrupt what has been continuous public fishing rights on the stream. There is limited access here. From East Koy Road to Babbitt Road and including the dam below, action is good near the bridges and fallen timber. Sometimes the *Isonychia* hatch is good and a size 10 Grey Wulff will produce spectacular results.

I've fished these areas since I was eight years old, and it's been a great, ongoing experience. I once watched the late Gaddabout Gaddis film a classic fishing adventure here, catching over 60 trout in a four hour filming sequence...and I became a believer in flies. Indeed, the fish are here. And today, there's more fish than ever before.

ISCHUA CREEK

Ischua Creek starts out in meadows and pastures and grows to a relatively large creek with changing stone and mud bottom structure. The upper creek supports brown trout, while the slower, downstream portions provide fishing opportunity for smallmouth and largemouth bass, northern pike, small musky and panfish. Located in Cattaraugus County, Ischua Creek follows Route 16, flowing south through Franklinville before ultimately meeting Oil Creek at Hinsdale and forming Olean Creek, which flows to the Allegany River.

Between 20,000 and 30,000 trout are stocked annually along its upper course. There are also a fair number of native browns. Public access totalling 11.5 miles is available along the river's 19.9 mile course.

There are public fishing areas between Route 242 and Route 16; above and below the intersections of Routes 98 and 16; and below Farewell Road for about one mile. This is a prime fly fishing stream, with good hatches of mayflies in May and June. Fly fishing at night with Muddler Minnows and dark streamers is a regular event on this stream, but fly fishing is not exclusive. Ultralight spinning gear and $\frac{1}{16}$ to $\frac{1}{8}$ ounce spinners, like Mepps and Panther Martins, are also productive.

UPPER GENESEE RIVER

From the dam at Belmont upstream to the Pennsylvania State Line (about 20 miles), the Upper Genesee River is managed as a trout stream. This section is stocked annually with about 4,400 rainbows and 22,000 brown trout. The entire section is open to trout fishing all year, with a daily creel limit of 5 trout.

Approximately 50 percent of the 10 mile section from Belmont to Wellsville has public fishing rights, and 80 percent of the 10 mile section from Wellsville to the state line has public access. A 2.5 mile section beginning at the Route 19 bridge in Shongo and going downstream is a no-kill area with artificial lures only permitted.

Paul Maciejewski of TU describes the upper Genesee as a

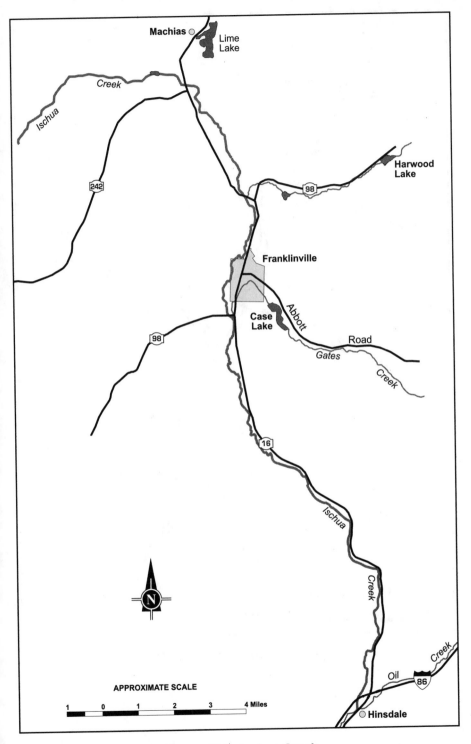

Figure 16.2   Ischua Creek

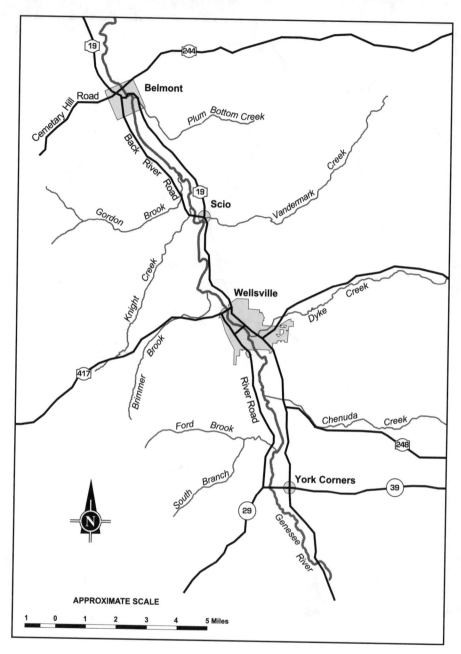

Figure 16.3   Upper Genesee River

perfect mix of water types, regardless of a trout fisherman's preference. The flows vary from riffles to flats, deep pools and white water, and often with slow runs in between. Brown trout are the chief residents, but the occasional rainbow and very occasional brook trout are here too.

Like most other trout waters in Western New York, insect life is varied. The most productive dry flies include caddis in the #14 to #18 range. The fish prefer grey, cream or rust, Light Cahills #12 to #18 as waters warm, and the Adams is an all around good choice of dry fly since it simulates so many different naturals. For the rough water, make sure you take along some good floater flies like the Humpy or any of the Wulff series. Later in the year, crickets, hoppers and ants will bring good action.

For the wet fly angler, caddis pupa, Light and Dark Cahills, Picket Pins and Hare's Ears in #8 to #16 work well. Small streamers like the Black Ghost and Grey Ghost also do a good job.

A fly rod with #4 to #6 weight line, in any length, is an effective tool on the Upper Genesee. Ultralight spinning anglers are successful with very light line of two to four pound test. Lighter line means more strikes, and I would rather say I caught eight out of 23 fish that hit than two out of two. Smaller spinners and spoons in lighter colors produce trout.

The Upper Genesee River drains a major watershed and before making a trip here, it may be wise to call to assure the river is not running high.

UPPER CATTARAUGUS CREEK

Upper Cattaraugus Creek flows through Ashford, Sardinia and Arcade, and offers early season action from a number of sites. The busy Route 16 bridge above Arcade is one of the most actively fished areas for early season anglers. There are carryover and some native brown trout, in addition to the 7,000 brown trout stocked in this stream each year.

The fish are normally stocked from the Yorkshire townline upstream to the Route 16 bridge. Over 13 miles of public access

exists on the stream, and all access sites are clearly marked. Stream width varies from 20 to 30 feet.

West Seneca resident Larry Wisher is an ultralight spinning expert on this water. Using #0 and #1 spinners, Wisher frequently catches five to ten trout in a dawn to 9 a.m. outing. He advises a silent approach and careful casting to the tails of pools; the riffles should also be fished. "Copper colored blades are a definite advantage at times," says Wisher.

TU member Bob Janiga advises that insect activity is predominately caddis, though a Grizzly King wet is a good searching pattern. The upper stream portions have good Mayfly hatches.

Access to the stream is available at Bixby Hill Road, West Avenue from Arcade, from Route 98 above East Arcade, and along Genesee Road and Cattaraugus Road.

Several tributaries of the Upper Cattaraugus Creek are also good. Among them are Hosmer Brook, Clear Creek, Spring Brook, Elton Creek, Lime Lake Outlet and McKinstry Creek. All of these are small streams, and several are stocked with fish each year.

Hosmer Brook is not stocked. There are native trout throughout the stream, but summer growth can make casting difficult. Public access is open from the mouth upstream to just above Route 39, about 1.5 miles.

Clear Creek has wild trout throughout its length. There is good access to much of this stream.

Elton Creek is stocked (2,900 browns) from the mouth upstream 4.2 miles. There is good access from the mouth upstream to the powerline crossing, totalling about 4 miles.

Lime Lake Outlet is managed as a wild trout stream along it's entire 4.5 mile stretch and has many public fishing areas.

Many of these streams contain holdover stocked trout, with some wild brown trout and native brook trout also present. Joe Evans, DEC Region 9 Senior Aquatic Biologist, advises

Fly fishing on the better streams of Western New York can be an intimate, rewarding experience.

that it can pay anglers to try the headwaters and tributaries to these waters. Look for forested sections with summer temperatures less than 65 degrees. Some may be wild goose chases, but you may just find your very own secret little piece of water where small but beautiful trout are abundant.

Chapter 17
THE FIVE BEST PONDS/LAKES IN DEC REGION 9
by David L. Barus

SILVER LAKE

Silver Lake is located in east-central Wyoming County, just south of Perry, New York. It currently supports a sport fishery made up of northern pike, largemouth bass, smallmouth bass and, to a lesser extent, walleye. There are also other fish of angler interest, namely, yellow perch, black crappie, brown bullhead, sunfish, and rock bass.

Silver Lake is unusual in that the inlet and outlet are both located on the north end of the lake, allowing the water to warm faster in spring and cool slower in the fall. The lake has a surface area of 762 acres, and it is shallow, with a maximum depth of 37 feet. It supports only a warm water fishery.

About three miles long and a half-mile wide, Silver Lake has a predominately mud bottom shaped like a big dish pan. There are no distinct holes, but there are sharp drop-offs, heavy weedbeds, a number of distinct gravel bars and other structure. These provide satisfactory cover for the large population of gamefish and forage species found here.

The extremely clear water of Silver Lake in spring allows sunlight to rapidly warm the shallows. The combination of rapidly warming water and ample oxygen promotes heavy weed growth along the shoreline. By summer, algae formation causes off-colored water, ideal for shallow water angling.

For many years, Silver Lake was known for its abundance of small panfish and yellow perch, mostly in the four to six inch range. Then in 1983, Silver Lake was selected for more intense management, including walleye stocking. Prior to this, only a remnant population of walleye existed here.

Production efforts shared between New York State and the Wyoming County Sportsmen's Federation were succesful. The walleye now control overabundant yellow perch and other panfish species. Yellow perch numbers are currently more balanced, and the fish are bigger, averaging seven to nine inches in size. These offer a tasty treat for fishermen to catch all through the year.

Perch are a favorite target of winter ice fishermen at Silver Lake. The winter perch can generally be found in 12 to 25 feet of water, on or near the bottom. Ice flies or ice jigs tipped with a mousie or spike grub, are worked within a foot or two of the bottom. Minnows also work well. A small bobber can be used as a visual aid and to suspend the bait at just the right distance from the bottom. Jiggle the line and let it set, keep an eye on the bobber for the slightest quiver and then repeat. Set the hook sharply at the first sign of a strike.

Occasional walleye are caught through the ice, as are northern pike and, more infrequently, crappie. Two hand lines and up to five tip-ups per angler may be used while ice fishing. All tip-ups must be marked with the name and address of the operator, and that person must be present when lines are in the water.

Beginning with ice out, schools of crappie move into the shallows at each end of Silver Lake and into the quiet bays along the east and west shoreline. These are best taken through the use of a bobber and suspended minnow. On certain days when the crappie move in, the water seems to turn dark with fish. Chris Perrinello, an expert local angler, says, "While many anglers use a jig and bobber rig, others use a wet streamer fly such as the Mickey Finn pattern to take crappie when they move into the canals at the north and south ends of the lake. When

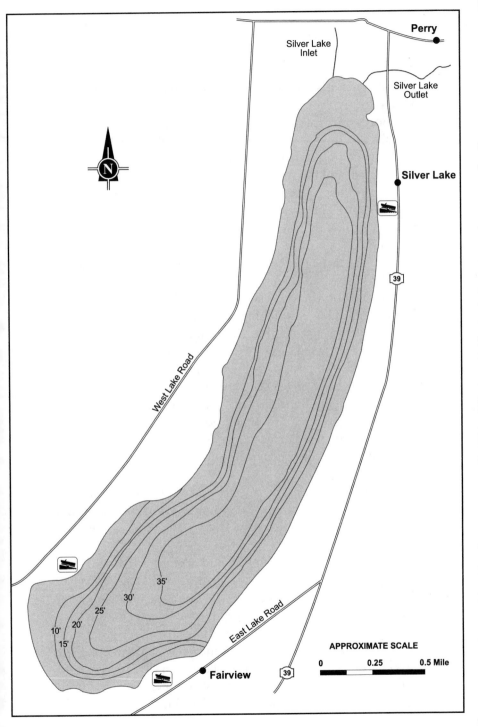

Figure 17.1   Silver Lake

the fish are in, it's not unusual to take dozens of ½ pound plus crappie from Silver Lake.

Shortly after ice out, yellow perch action also picks up. Local veterans use tiny ¹⁄₃₂ or ¹⁄₁₆ ounce plastic-tailed jigs fished in a very slow jigging style near the bottom. Purple is always a hot color jig tail, and the small, 1½ inch or 2 inch sizes are favored.

On the first Saturday in May, walleye and northern pike season opens. There are some hefty northerns in Silver Lake. Every year, Jim and Jane Bellamy at Silver Lake Marine run a contest on opening day. The winning pike may weigh 15 pounds or more. The tactic for these bigger fish has remained unchanged over the years, and involves fishing six to eight inch suckers right on the bottom with a slip sinker (no bobber). Simply keep your eye on the line, watching for it to move off. You have to wait a while for a strike, but the resulting trophy is worth it. Smaller pike are taken casting #9 red and white Dardevle spoons and #4 or #5 spinnerbaits over emerging weedbeds.

The walleye at Silver Lake are taken in a number of ways. Casting or trolling Rapalas at twilight is a favored method, but casting and working a ¼ ounce lead-head jig is also effective. As waters warm, the fish move into the weedline. Anglers drifting spinner and worm rigs or jigs tipped with a small piece of worm are successful.

Veteran bass anglers occasionally take largemouths to seven pounds and smallmouths to five pounds from Silver Lake. But more typical are bass in the one to two pound range for both species.

Plastic worms worked under and around docks are effective for largemouth bass, as are floating crankbaits twitched and pumped on the surface at dawn and dusk. Buzzbait spinners worked over weedbeds are productive for largemouth bass, and an occasional northern may hammer them as well.

Traditional jig and pig (pork rind) rigs worked along the gravel bars found on the central east shore of the lake will call a smallmouth bass to breakfast on most summer days. And trolling with small, diving crankbaits is also productive when the baits are trailed just outside the weedline. Use Rebels, Wiggle-Warts and similar lures. Unfortunately, the heavy weed conditions of mid-summer normally discourages this type of fishing. But autumn trolling over subsiding weeds can be memorable.

Access to Silver Lake is excellent. A concrete ramp at Silver Lake Marine, located in the southwest corner of the lake, will handle boats to 24 feet. Mack's Boat Livery is situated on the southeast corner, and Tucker's Boat Livery is on the east shore. Koziel's Livery is on Oatka Road at the lake inlet. In the far southwest corner, there is a state-owned cartop only launch area.

CUBA LAKE

Cuba Lake is a 493 acre reservoir formed in the 1850s by the damming of Oil Creek. Situated in west-central Allegany County, some 17 miles north of the Pennsylvania State line, it is a popular water for largemouth and smallmouth bass, walleye, yellow perch, rock bass, crappie, tiger muskellunge and other panfish.

The most abundant gamefish species in Cuba Lake is the walleye. The DEC has expended considerable effort to enhance the walleye population here. For many years, DEC stocked as many as 2½ million walleye fry per year. Despite the high stocking levels, walleye are considered hard to catch. The abundance of weed growth and forage fish seems to be the reason. Weedbeds, primarily millfoil, surround a majority of the western and southern shorelines, providing excellent cover. The weeds are home for walleye, largemouth bass and yellow perch.

The largemouth bass will tear up surface stickbaits (three to five inch Rebel or Rapala style lures) and six inch, purple or brown colored plastic worms skittered along the top of the millfoil edges. Live bait under bobbers is your best bet for walleye and perch.

The north and eastern shores of the lake provide good habitat for smallmouth bass and fair numbers of walleye. Rubble and gravel bars are numerous here. Crabs and minnows fished over the bars can yield excellent results. Veteran anglers work

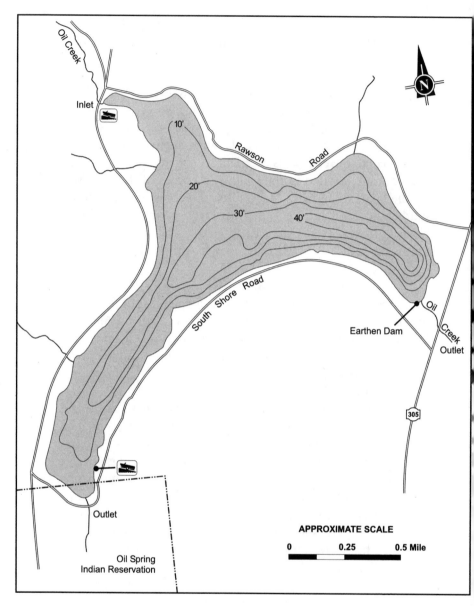

Figure 17.2 Cuba Lake

$^1/_4$ to $^3/_8$ ounce black hair jigs along the bars with equally effective catch rates.Boat access is primarily for small craft of less than 18 feet. There are two free launches available for public use. One is near the spillway on South Shore Road and the other is on West Shore Road at the Oil Creek inlet.

Ice Fishing has long been popular on Cuba Lake. Favored areas include the deep waters near the dam. Ice flies and grubs near the bottom work well.

The warmth of summer, and August in particular, causes low oxygen levels in the deeper waters of the lake. Because of this, fish will relocate to the shallow areas of the lake.

Cuba Lake is lined with cottages, but it still remains a popular "little lake" for anglers that are willing to travel to its shores.

CASE LAKE

Case Lake is situated in Cattaraugus County on Abbotts Road, just east of Franklinville. The lake was formed many years ago by an earthen dam placed across Gates Creek for flood control purposes. It is now managed for secondary recreational purposes by the DEC. Case Lake provides great opportunity in a scenic setting that enhances the fishing experience.

The 80-acre impoundment is stocked annually with brown and rainbow trout. These provide ready excitement for youngsters fishing the inlet after ice-out. Worms, bits of corn or chopped liver, fished off a bobber or on the bottom, will catch the smaller hatchery sized fish. There is no minimum size limit and no closed season for trout on Case Lake, but the creel limit is five trout per day.

To entertain more serious anglers, excess breeder brown and rainbow trout are regularly stocked. These fish are released at sizes up to ten pounds and 30 inches in length.

Besides trout, the lake supports a warm water fishery of largemouth bass and panfish. Occasional bass to five pounds are caught here, but the average is much smaller.

Flycasters enjoy success with a variety of wet fly, dry fly and streamer presentations. Top wet fly patterns include the Hare's

Ear, Leadwing Coachmen, and Gold-Ribbed Brown Hackle in #12 to #14 sizes. The best dry fly patterns include the Quill Gordon, Blue Dun and Light Cahill in #12 to #14 sizes. The top streamer pattern is the #6 Muddler Minnow with silver tinsel on a 3XL hook; the Grey Ghost pattern is a close second.

Canoeists and those who utilize Case Lake from a small cartop boat can effectively fish the deep drop-offs found along Abbotts Road on the northeast shoreline with spincast or ultralight spinning outfits. Casters use many lures here, and $\frac{1}{16}$ ounce to $\frac{1}{8}$ ounce plastic-tailed jigs in white or chartreuse colors are proven fish catchers.

Shore casters enjoy success with small #0 and #1 spinners. The tiny spinners can be tough to cast on a windy day, but you can always move to the other side of the lake. The Mepps Wooly-Worm, an ultralight spinner in $\frac{1}{18}$ ounce size is an excellent choice for Case Lake. There have been times when I have caught six to 10 fish per hour while using this spinner pattern.

The upper end of the lake near the Gates Creek inlet is shallow, and in summer heavy weedbeds offer perfect cover for big bass. Small top water stickbaits are effective when worked slowly over the holes found in the dense weedbeds at dawn and dusk. Proven Case Lake stickbaits include size #F-7 and #F-9 Rapalas.

No gasoline motors are allowed on the lake, but cartops, rowboats and canoes are permitted. These may be powered with electric motors. There is no ramp, but a cartop launch area with public parking is located directly off Abbotts Road. This is also the location of the lake's picnic complex. Camping is not permitted.

Case Lake is one of the few managed lakes that permit ice fishing. There is also no restriction regarding the use of live or dead bait. But check your regulations before fishing to assure there are no changes.

CASSADAGA LAKE

Cassadaga Lake is a scenic chain of three natural lakes situated in the towns of Pomfret and Stockton in north-central Chautauqua County. The lakes are fed by small streams and underwater springs. The primary outlet, Cassadaga Creek, empties into the Allegany River.

The lakes have historically been managed by the DEC as a warm water fishery, with muskellunge as the primary predator. Other gamefish found in the Cassadaga Lake chain include largemouth and smallmouth bass, yellow perch, northern pike, bullheads, numerous panfish including black and white crappie, and also a small number of walleye. Carp, while normally not considered a gamefish, are also found here, and are a popular species with bow fishing enthusiasts.

The lakes are classed as kettle lakes, meaning they were formed by parts of glaciers being buried in the ground. When the glaciers melted, the lakes remained. The upper lake is approximately 100 acres in size and has a maximum depth of 35 feet. The middle lake is some 25 acres with a depth of 35 feet. And the lower lake is approximately 100 acres and has the greatest depth, 54 feet. In each of the three lakes there are literally hundreds of structure and sub-structure bottom configurations.

Springtime means crappie fishing at Cassadaga. Depending on wind and sky conditions, spawning crappie generally locate in the warmest water they can find. Stick to any of the shallow bays that are out of the wind. Minnow and bobber or jig and bobber rigs will effectively take crappie. The best action starts around the third week in April. Don't give up if fish are not found at the first stop. Just try another shallow bay. Cast out and retrieve slowly, stop and retrieve again.

Cassadaga muskellunge love to cruise through the cabbage weed patches. Cast or troll these areas for success. The sulking, unpredictable behavior of Cassadaga muskies is one reason why anglers have always been intrigued by this toothy predator. Fish are their favorite food, and crappie, perch and other panfish species at Cassadaga make up much of the musky diet. Early morning musky meals can also include frogs, mice, rats, ducklings, snakes and other "forage."

Use a stout rod with 17 to 30 pound dacron line for abrasion resistance, and add a 12 inch wire leader for additional security. Eight to ten inch jerkbaits, large #4 and #5 spinners, and specially made bucktails are excellent baits for the serious musky angler. Keep the hooks razor sharp to better penetrate the bony jaw.

Look for largemouth bass off the underwater points and weedbeds. The fish will drift up and down the slope of the structure to feed in shallower water at dawn and again at dusk periods. If a bed of cornstalk-like weeds (sharp-fruited rush) intersects the main weedbed, key on this structure to find fish. Plastic worms in purple or blue, in the six or seven inch size, are effective. So are stickbaits. Largemouth will attack any surface disturbance that looks like food. That's one reason why they are so much fun to catch.

At each of the lake connections, there are distinct humps and flats. Each of these areas is a good feeding area and a potential inter-lake migration lane. Don't overlook these fishing territories. Utilize a depth sounder and a handful of floating markers to define potentially productive fishing areas in a systematic way.

Smallmouth bass can likewise be found near sand or gravel underwater points and where small shoals or underwater islands are noted. The southeast shore of the upper lake as it exits to the middle lake has ideal smallmouth structure.

Most of the northern pike caught are taken by anglers fishing for largemouth bass or musky. Some northerns reach 40 inches at Cassadaga Lake, with 30 plus inches fairly common.

Northerns may also be taken through the ice. Note, though the lower basin has some fairly deep holes, and ice above these areas tends to take longer to freeze. Exercise caution.

A public access area and launch is maintained by the state off Route 60 on the middle lake. There is no fee. The site will accommodate medium sized boats.

In the ponds and lakes of Region 9, warm weather fishing and hard water angling can both be enjoyed.

WATERPORT POND/LAKE ALICE

Waterport Pond, also known as Lake Alice, is located in central Orleans County. It is a 340 acre artificial impoundment, created in the 1930s when a hydroelectric powerplant was constructed on Oak Orchard Creek. To this day, the powerplant is maintained and operated by Niagara Mohawk, and lake levels are controlled by an agreement between Ni-Mo and the DEC.

As a high school youngster, I came to know Waterport Pond as more than just a small lake. It was the beginning of a life-long relationship.

Waterport was a place where big fish could potentially be caught on any cast. Local anglers all told stories of "the big one that got away" and, as I learned over the next 30 years, they weren't fooling! Largemouth bass up to eight pounds have been taken from "the pond," as have smallmouth over five pounds and northern pike over 18 pounds. There are also some walleye, an excellent population of black crappie that can reach a pound, yellow perch, white perch and several other panfish, including rock bass.

The lake is situated in an east-west canyon of slate walls, many of them nearly vertical. The steepest bluffs are found along the northern bank of the reservoir, with smaller bluff structure found on the southern exposure. Adjacent to the cliff-like bluffs excellent bottom structure can be found in the form of gently descending lake bottom that eventually comes to an underwater cliff. Warm water fish of all species lay along these areas, especially where an adjacent weedbed can be found.

In addition to the shore bluffs and corresponding deep drop-offs, there is an abundance of other structure. Intersecting creek channels, major underwater points, old sunken roadbeds and buildings, sunken tree trunks, gravel shoals, islands and enormous weedbeds are all a part of the fish's habitat. Each year more trees fall from the bluffs (generally large red oaks) and create new fishing hotspots.

Action begins each spring with the first ice melt. Large schools of white perch move onto the mud flats in the coves around the lake. These tasty little fish love small worms. Using a two hook bottom rig, just cast and wait, randomly retrieving the line once in a while. While only a panfish, the white perch hits hard and fast, and will surprise the unsuspecting angler when caught. They are generally taken in good numbers around the same time the first runs of brown bullheads occur.

A few weeks later, about the third week in April, huge schools of black crappie move into the same areas where the bullheads and white perch were.

The crappie at Waterport often suspend two to four feet down over five to eight feet of water to soak up the warmth of that spring sunshine. They will congregate around the numerous fallen tree structures along the shoreline perimeter. Look for them, too, over gravel and sand bottom areas in three to five feet of water where weeds are emerging. The spring fishing rig for crappie consists of a simple bobber and a suspended jig. You might use live bait under the same bobber. Bait or lure, either should be set to run 2 to 4 feet below the surface.

After a crappie school is found, the bobber can be removed and a jig simply cast and slowly retrieved over the fish. The strike is soft, the fish only mouth the jig and swim slowly away. Watch your line to detect this and then just lift the rod gently. Don't set the hook hard on these paper-mouthed fish.

Especially good areas for spring crappie on Waterport include the Otter Creek cove and the backwater flats found there; the slough on the northwest corner of the Kenyonville Road bridge; and the "stumps", about one mile west and around the first major upstream bend above the Kenyonville bridge. The "stumps" occupy an area of several acres, and are situated right in the middle of the creekbed. There are no markers on them, so be careful when approaching by boat.

Surface crappie action will last until June, when the fish slide down the structure to new depths.

The northern pike opener in May is a special time at Waterport. Oak Orchard Creek is well noted for lunker northern pike, and Waterport Pond is the best natural spawning ground for these freshwater monsters. Anglers fish both from shore and boats. Bobbers with suspended chubs or six to eight inch suckers take a good number of big northerns every year. Cast into the quiet waters along the coves, mud flats and emerging weedbeds for best action. The water may be still too cold for consistent success with spoon, plug and spinner presentations, but by the end of May the artificial lures are effective.

Educated bass anglers work with hi-tech bass boats, but many weekend anglers travel to Waterport Pond just to fish it

Sunfish inhabit nearly every pond and lake in the region, and many streams and rivers as well. Unknown to many people, sunfish (which include bluegills) are very good eating – especially when taken from cold water.

from a canoe or cartop boat. It's very relaxing that way, but do it early before the water skiers wake up.

Favored techniques for late June and early July bass are numerous. My cousins, Tom and Don Warda, have taken a great number of bass by working surface weedbeds with a plastic frog or a rubber worm on a weedless size 4/0 hook. They have caught bass to five pounds with regularity. Morning fishing stints are preferred for this weed habitat. Simply cast the frog from the boat to shore. Landing it on shore doesn't hurt anything. Hop it in, and let it set there for about five seconds. Then just wiggle it, but only enough to make the top of the weeds quiver without really moving the frog. It will entice any bass within 10 yards.

One favorite method of fishing Waterport can be observed on any Sunday afternoon by taking a short drive across the Eagle-Harbor, Route 279 bridge. You'll see dozens of anglers leaning over the bridge. It will appear they are looking for something that fell in, but actually, they are dabbling a two inch minnow, carefully hooked through the lips of an Eagle Claw Model 202 thin-wire hook. Attached to the line will be a BB-shot some 18 inches above the bait. Anglers drift the minnow 15 feet to 20 feet down into the depths near the bridge abutments. Crappie lying in the shadow of the bridge and just above the edge of the thermocline will creep upward and suck the minnow in for a quick meal. Anglers catch as many as three or four dozen fish with this toss-and-fall technique. Other bridges that cross the lake also permit anglers to find and catch crappie in the same manner.

Public boat access has been improved by the Orleans County Federation of Sportsmen. A revamped launch and parking area is situated on the north shore of the impoundment, just across the Route 279 bridge. There is no fee for use of the ramp.

Ice fishing is permitted on Waterport and can be very good at times. Crappie, bluegills, yellow perch and northern pike are all frequently caught. Work the areas over 10 to 23 feet of water, generally along what was the summer weedline, for good success.

Chapter 18
CHAUTAUQUA LAKE
by David L. Barus

F or the weekend angler or more serious fisherman, Chautauqua Lake is one of those special fishing places that you can never remove from your mind. Shallow water, deep water, weed lines, shoal structure, underwater islands, sunken points, docks, irregular shape -- Chautauqua has it all!

Chautauqua offers fine fishing, especially for walleye, crappie and smallmouth bass. But largemouth bass, yellow perch, brown bullhead, other panfish species, and the occasional once in a lifetime trophy musky make the prospects most exciting.

Nestled in the picturesque, southwest corner of New York State, Chautauqua Lake is a natural, fertile lake some 17 miles in length, but averaging only about one mile in width. With the Lake Erie shoreline so near, it is somewhat surprising that the geography of the area is such that no outflow from Chautauqua Lake ever reaches Lake Erie. Rather, the outflow is in the opposite direction through Jamestown, down the Chadakoin River and eventually to the Allegany River. Inlet waters to Chautauqua consist of a few small streams that run off the hillsides, and numerous springs found throughout the lake bottom.

Fishing is diversified, and available from shore or boat. An angler can practice his preferred pastime with a cane pole, trolling rod, fly rod or ultralight rig with hair-thin monofilament line, or in any of a hundred other ways. And here, you never know when a wall-hanger may latch onto your line.

Chautauqua is an Indian name meaning "bag tied in the middle." The middle of the "bag" is at Bemus Point, an area that serves to separate the lake into two distinctly different halves.

At Bemus Point, a car ferry still operates during summer months to transfer vacationing anglers across the lake. It is more a special experience than logical transportation. The ferry was outdated on an official basis by the new I-86 bridge, a high-rise structure that stands in view of the ferry landing. The bridge crosses the lake just to the east of Bemus Point. The huge bridge pillars offer excellent fishing structure, especially for crappie in mid-May.

The northwestern portion of the lake from Bemus Point to Mayville, or the "upper end" as local folks call it, is relatively deep. The water here is generally clear with an average depth of about 30 feet, but there are some eight separate holes ranging in depth down to 77 feet, and each hole will attract walleye at various times of year.

The bottom structure of this upper end is mainly gravel, sand and rubble, with a subtle weedline that exists around the lake perimeter at roughly 12 feet of depth. This excellent combination of structure and weeds helps balance the needs of both forage and gamefish throughout the year. The deeper holes offer cool refuge to gamefish during the periods of summer heat, when a thermocline will form. Similarly, the holes usually offer exceptional fall and winter walleye action after fall turnover.

The southeastern end of the lake from Bemus Point to Jamestown, the "lower end," is much shallower and averages only 15 feet in depth. There are no significant holes here. The deepest spot is a mere 19 feet, a gentle, sloping dish pan shape about 300 yards long. It is parallel to and about 300 yards off the north shore, directly opposite Cheney's Point.

The lower end offers big weedbeds along each shoreline and a bottom composed mostly of mud, muck and sand. The water is more turbid in summer, but still semi-transparent. The extreme lower end toward Jamestown offers numerous gravel shoals combined with heavy weed growth.

Lakewood Bar, for example, is an excellent shoal attracting many species of gamefish. Bass, crappie and walleye are found near this hotspot throughout the year. It is situated on the south shore, off the first point to the right coming from Asheville Bay. It is basically an oval shape, yet is irregular in spots, pointing toward the center of the lake from the point.

Other shoals in the lower end include the Middle-Lake Shoals, a series of high spots located farther south of Lakewood Bar and closer to the north shore. These are also excellent areas to fish. These shoals are so shallow (three feet or less) that they are marked by buoys, making the job of locating them that much easier for anglers. In fact, there are buoys strategically placed by the DEC during the ice-free time of the year on most of the shoals, points and other areas that pose a danger to boaters.

While Chautauqua Lake was historically famous for musky action, and these toothy fighters are still a part of Chautauqua fishing activity, the walleye is now the focal point of most fishing. Crappie and bass angling run a close second. Numerous tournaments are held on Chautauqua Lake for each of these gamefish species.

Trophy-sized crappie can tilt the scales at just under three pounds, with average weights generally in the ½ to ¾ pound range. Smallmouth bass average about one to two pounds, but seven pound monsters are caught here every year in September and October. Largemouth bass will reach six pounds plus. A trophy walleye will be 11 to 13 pounds, while the average walleye is about two pounds.

Walleye are not native to Chautauqua Lake, and how they actually reached Chautauqua is an unsolved mystery. They were not stocked by the fishery folks at the DEC, who surmise the introduction of walleye actually occurred sometime in the late 1950s.

The walleye numbers in Chautauqua Lake today are unheralded. It is the newest walleye frontier in the northeast, and fishing action, either from shore or by boat, gets better with every passing season.

Natural walleye spawning occurs in the small stream inlets during March and April, before the season for the species is open. Many walleye will not make these runs, but instead spawn along the many miles of sand shallows located in the quiet bays around the periphery of the lake.

When the season opens, the best walleye catches are made at dusk and just after dark. Anglers flipping F-9 or F-11 Rapalas in three to seven feet of water do best. Any color seems to work, though many anglers seem to prefer silver and black. You can fish from a boat, wade or cast from docks, shore points and piers.

One especially productive early season walleye area for shore casters is on the Stow (south) side of the Bemus Ferry landing. My good fishing friend Roger Miller, proprietor of Lakeside Fishing Cottages adjacent to the Stow landing will, on a good day, hook and land five keeper walleye from one to three pounds and at least one musky while casting from shore. Miller regularly tosses five and six pound walleye in the cooler from the same location. The action lasts throughout the month of May.

Night casting for walleye is fun. The lack of motor trolling noise is a bonus, making the experience all the more enjoyable. Wear a hat light or carry a flashlight to aid in knot tying, landing fish and getting your bearings after dark.

For this kind of fishing, a 5½ foot ultralight graphite rod with a lightweight reel and four pound monofilament line is ideal. Just be sure to check your reel's drag before casting. It's not unusual to hook a musky during this type of fishing, so be prepared!

After dark the upper end of the lake transforms into a virtual city of lights. Weekends will find the night lake dotted with hundreds of red, green and white running lights as anglers troll the shallows after dark. Rapalas, Rebels, Junior Thundersticks, and the like make up the majority of lures that perform well on Chautauqua. Periodically, jointed lures like

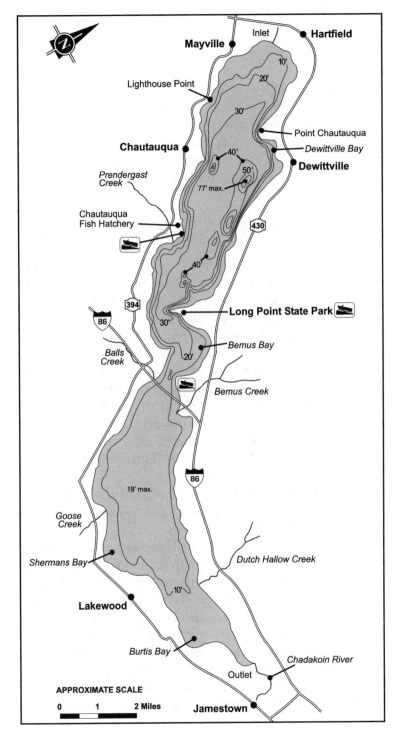

Figure 18.1   Chautauqua Lake

the J-9 Rapala and similar lures this size, in perch or chartreuse finish, become the hot night time trolling plugs. The important thing is to stay in depths of five to seven feet of water. You might also attach a ⅛ ounce split shot about two feet ahead of the lure to keep you near the bottom and to keep weeds off the lure. That's a key element. You'll still have to clean your lure occasionally.

Trolling speeds are slow, typically less than two miles per hour. Another important issue is to stay quiet. Local anglers prefer to troll with silent running electric motors for improved success.

While going slow is usually the golden rule at night, when it doesn't work move the throttle up to three, four or even 4½ miles per hour. Bigger electric motors will propel to this speed with little problem, and you'll find big walleye can easily snatch the lure at these high speeds. An odd musky may be provoked into striking too.

Key trolling locations include almost every part of the upper lake shoreline. The most popular trolling areas include the inside weedlines: from just north of the Bell Tower at Chautauqua Institute northward toward Lighthouse Point (in the direction of Mayville); off the mouth of Dewittville Bay southward to Mission Meadows; and off Prendergast Bay southward toward the Magnolia gravel bars.

There are many areas in the south end too, but anglers trolling plugs prefer the upper end due to cooler waters and the lack of weed growth during May.

Casters can really score on walleyes on the lower (south) end of the lake by casting to the quiet waters near the shoals and along any of the gravel-bottomed bays during the early evening darkness. Bly Bay is a good drift-and-cast spot for boaters; shallow water wading can also be practiced here.

During the daylight hours of May, early season walleye tend to move to the edge of thickening weedlines and near the end of the many bars in the lake. In the upper end, fish near Warner Bar, off Mission Meadows and off the Bell Tower. Fish can be caught by working vertical jigging lures like Silver Buddys,

Sonars, Rapala ice-jigging lures, Mepp's Syclops and the like. A slowly drifted spinner and worm along the weedline will also produce walleye strikes. These fish will be mostly males, but occasional large females will also hit.

By June, the fish have left the nearshore shallows and moved to a more comfortable and secure residence along the emerging weedbeds. As summer arrives, water temperatures climb and a thermocline forms by July in the upper end. Water becomes very warm in the lower end, promoting both algae growth and murkiness. Some gamefish migrate to the deeper, upper end of the lake as summer progresses. Summer walleye move into the shade of the weeds and into the depths of the upper end holes.

One effective way to fish the weeds is by a method called "jig dropping." Simply move your boat quietly with either an electric motor or sculling oar while looking for holes in the weeds. Position the boat five to six feet off the hole and drop a ¼ to ⅜ ounce jig into it. Hair or plastic tail jigs both work. The water is not deep, only five to eight feet, so it won't take long for the jig to reach the bottom. When it does, lift it up with a solid jerk. If a fish is there, he will have inhaled the jig on the fall and immediately be hooked when you lift up. Try this summer technique if you have never done so. It seems to work best when the weeds first develop and the water warms, but it is still productive later when the fish seem to get lazy and more finicky. I've had excellent success with Blockbuster brand jigs, manufactured locally by Dave Bianchi, who is also actively associated with the New York Walleye Association.

As the weather cools in autumn, Chautauqua Lake walleye fishing starts to heat up. The cooling surface waters sink toward the bottom, creating the start of lake turnover. The water inversion occurs in the shallower, lower end of the lake first, prompting the lower end walleyes to find favorable temperatures and clear water in the upper lake. Then a few weeks later, the upper lake also turns over. After turnover, the walleye concentrate near the bottom in the upper end holes. They begin to gorge themselves before winter, and anglers tossing vertical jigging hardware clean up.

Will Elliott, a local angling expert, has taken as many as 70 walleye in an afternoon while fishing three to a boat. He uses barbless hooks to minimize damage to the fish and promote easy and quick releases. Of course he keeps no more than his limit of five fish per trip.

Any type of vertical jigging hardware is effective, although certain days seem to require a specific color or size. Chartreuse, blue and green are popular colors.

Of course walleye will also take live minnows, chubs and worms at this time. Russ Johnson, another local expert, uses golden shiners fished on the bottom to catch big walleyes. Other successful anglers will use worm-tipped jigs fished from a slow backtroll (with electric motor) along the hole edges to harvest late season walleye. A slow twitch, a gentle flip, then a short pause constitute a good technique.

Every fall after turnover thousands of walleye are found holding in the hole off Long Point. An angler can easily tell when fishing is best in fall. It always peaks when deer season opens and continues right until ice-up.

Once the ice is solidly formed, a whole new fishing arena is available. If you fished the lake in summer and remember where you saw big pockets in the weeds, this is where you want to fish now. On sunny winter days, early and late in the ice fishing season, these areas warm first and are good spots for fishing activity.

On the overcast days, and as winter moves on through January, key fishing locations become the vertical drops that surround the deep hole areas of the upper end. Jigging spoons tipped with a minnow are preferred. Number 7 and 9 Swedish Pimples, W-9 and W-11 Rapalas, and other similar lures will all produce fish. Lower the lure to the bottom, then lift the rod

Crappies are the trophy fish of winter on Chautauqua Lake.
(Courtesy State Tourism Office)

six to 12 inches. Let the lure fall, watching the rod tip. Repeat for at least five minutes, then vary the retrieve style. You might twitch the lure or lift it two feet or more, but always watch the rod tip. Any change in the feel of the lure will signify a strike. Set the hook!

Veteran anglers will use two rods at a time, doubling his chances, in holes drilled five to six feet apart. Working the rods alternately, an angler can quickly see if the area being fished is productive or not. If it's not producing fish after ten minutes, move or change lures. Move 100 feet out, 100 feet in, but change.

Many Chautauqua anglers also ice fish for walleye and perch using live minnows off tip-ups. The use of tip-ups lets you spread out more and find fish faster. Normally you will want at least 50 feet between your holes to give you the best chance of finding a school of fish. Anglers will often start to hand-jig the better producing hole while still watching for their flags.

Keep your eyes open for what's going on around you. If you're not watching, the guy right behind you could be catching 10 walleyes on a Swedish Pimple while you are zapped with a jigging Rapala, or vice versa. Most times it's more the location of your hole than anything else. A certain amount of local intelligence gathering is fundamental to success.

Crappie fishing in Chautauqua begins soon after ice out. Kids, parents, grandpa and grandma – everyone joins in the fun of catching these tasty panfish when the early fish swim into the canals at the lower end of the lake.

Look for spring crappie around any submerged pilings, docks, underwater obstructions, boat slips and the like. Use live minnows hooked through the lips or 1/32 ounce jigs. Set either the bait or jig two to four feet below a low-resistance quill or small foam bobber. Cast out and retrieve very slowly, stopping the rig periodically. The fish generally strike during the pause. They won't hammer the bait or jig, but instead will slowly grab it and move off. Let them run for three or four seconds and then gently lift the rod to hook these soft-mouthed fish. Preferred jig tail colors include chartreuse, yellow, white or black.

The key variables for successful crappie fishing are the retrieve speed and depth from the surface that these fish are lingering. Crappie like to suspend in a comfort zone. In spring, this means catching the warm rays of spring sunshine. In summer, it means getting your bait just beyond the depth of sun ray penetration.

In spring, small but savory crappie can often be found in schools two feet down in eight to 10 feet of water. Though the suspended depth varies with the amount of sun, a good number of bigger, early season crappie lurk in the five to 10 foot depths a little farther offshore from where the smaller fish are found. For this deeper fishing, a slip bobber is great. Set it at the desired depth and go to it.

With either the slip bobber or fixed bobber, remember to fan cast around the boat, working the entire area to find fish. They will often school very tightly, and can be difficult to locate. Once found, it's not unusual to take 50 fish from the same little pocket.

Summer crappie roam the weedlines and are considered hard to catch mainly because they are deeper. The slip bobber will still work at this time. Look for crappie where a series of cornstalk (rush) weeds can be found in 10 to 15 feet of water. As waters cool in fall, the crappie will again move to the shallows, and can be caught with the same spring tactics.

Please note that the daily creel limit of crappie on Chautauqua Lake has been reduced from unlimited to 25 fish per person per day. Check the current fishing regulations for possible changes of this or any other law governing fishing on this lake.

Musky season opens with bass season in June, and the fish are ready to do battle at this time. While recent years have seen a slight decline in the abundance of this powerful gamefish, the musky hatchery on the lake at Prendergast Point will help to maintain the presence of this great game fish.

Some anglers blame the decline of the musky on the massive increase of large walleye, but the exact reason is unknown. Good musky fishing will generally last from the opener through the end of July. It falls off during the hot summer period, then picks up again with the first frost.

Trolling large stick lures like magnum Rapala minnows, Pikie Minnows, Creek Chub and similar lures is very popular. Warren Berry, an old friend and former musky guide on Chautauqua, will often tempt these freshwater monsters to strike by trolling his lures very close to the wake of the motor. But for most anglers, a long line is the norm. Downriggers are also used during the summer months for controlled depth trolling. Other anglers use big spoons or Mepps Musky Killer spinners cast near shore structure early in the day or in the evening.

The minimum musky length at Chautauqua is 40 inches, and you are limited to one fish per day. The lake record weighed 51 pounds, 3 ounces but the average musky is under 20 pounds. Anglers are encouraged to release these fish.

Chautauqua has abundant numbers of both largemouth and smallmouth bass, and real trophy smallmouth are possible. In the early season, look for smallmouth around rock piles, the many underwater bars around the lake and off most points. Traditional baits and lures will bring success. As the season progresses, these bass move deeper and drifting with crayfish is more productive.

Largemouth bass prefer the weedier areas in shallow water. Plastic grubs, jigs and worms, as well as topwater stickbaits are all productive. Best fishing times for either species are dawn and dusk.

Public access for shore fishing on Chautauqua is good. Popular shore areas are: Mayville Town Park at the northwest corner of the lake; Prendergast Point on the south shore off Route 394 seven miles south of Mayville; Long Point State Park on the north shore near the middle of the lake off I-86; Bemus Point Ferry Landing at the narrows near the middle of the lake on both the north and south shores; Stow Ferry Landing on the eastern shore at mid-lake; and Dunham Avenue on the lower shore at Celeron.

There are numerous boat launch sites. Prendergast Point, off Route 394, has been refurbished recently. This site now provides modern concrete ramps with ample parking, all in a park-like setting complete with picnic tables. No boat gas or electricity is available at this site. Long Point (Chautauqua Lake State Park) off Route 430 on the north shore near Bemus Point, is a full service marina, including slips for transient boaters. Long Point is the most popular launch on Chautauqua Lake. This site is relatively protected from a southwest or northwest wind. Bemus Point, in the village of Bemus Point, has a small launch for boats less than 16 feet. The site offers limited parking.

There are numerous privately owned boat launches at various marinas around the perimeter of the lake. Many of these also have boat rentals.

INDEX

A

B

C

K

L

M

N

O

P